AGGRESSIVE POSITIVITY™

Fearlessly Actioning a Positive Present and Future

D1409112

By Limore

Cover & Logo Design by Rony Freiman at ShapeMediaDesigns

Book Design by Limore Zisckind

Editing by Michael Melnick

First Printing, 2020

ISBN 9798633858433

"Imagine you could open your eyes to see only the good in every person, the positive in every circumstance, and the opportunity in every challenge."

-Rabbi M.M. Shneerson

CONTENTS

I would like to dedicate this book to my husband, children, parents, siblings, in-laws, nieces, nephews, friends, family, present and future generations.

I would also like to dedicate this book in loving memory of Jenny Lewis, my high school colleague.

FOREWORD

I first met Limore before her cancer diagnosis, when she so generously volunteered to perform at a fundraiser for PYNK, a program at our hospital that offers special support to young breast cancer patients and their families. Limore's performance was not only artistically superb, but gave our event a special boost of energy and positivity with her youthful exuberance. Who would have thought that just over a year later she would become a PYNK "client" and my patient?

Perhaps the most difficult aspect of a cancer diagnosis is that, by its very nature, the disease signifies loss of control for the patient. Many patients struggle to find some aspect over which they do have control and may embrace restrictive diets or ingest copious 'supplements' of unproven benefit. Limore's philosophy of "aggressive positivity" offers an alternative that may or may not have any impact on the disease's prognosis but will inevitably improve any cancer patient's quality of life, not only during treatment but indefinitely.

Patients who have approached their disease in a similar way have told me that cancer diagnosis ultimately made them much happier people by providing them with the impetus to cast off much of the negativity in their lives (e.g. a stressful job, an abusive relationship, etc.) and to become more mindful of and grateful for the good things.

Over the course of my career I've read many books written by cancer patients about their so-called "cancer journey." These books range from simple blogs to beautifully crafted literary works. Yet all focus on the patient and his or her cancer.

Although "Aggressive Positivity™" was written by a cancer patient and her breast cancer is a dominant character, the book (just like the uplifting words on its cover) is not about cancer. It's a book about choice, health, and life, packaged in an easy-reading style the length of a magazine article. So, if you're planning to give this to a friend with cancer - read it first! Better yet, keep a copy for yourself. Its universal messages are a perfect prescription for dealing with any major challenge.

By Dr. Ellen Warner MD, FRCPC, FACP, M. Sc, world renowned medical oncologist and affiliate scientist

INTRODUCTION

Thank you for coming on this journey with me!

I wanted to write a brief, concise, and useful guide to help you get through difficult challenges. It shouldn't take you very long to read this book, but hopefully you will come away with new perspectives or skills to apply to your everyday life.

The principles of Aggressive Positivity are simple to understand. I don't pretend to have the answers to everything, but I do feel compelled to share how I managed to face a monster - my breast cancer diagnosis and subsequent treatment - with fearless optimism and action.

Do not be fooled by my smile - it took significant and consistent efforts to achieve - but it does get easier with practice. I am only human. I get sad, angry, afraid and self-conscious like everyone. What I do with those kinds of emotions is what I am here to share.

Feel free to adapt what I did to suit your needs and carve your own   way.

Practicing Aggressive Positivity is a choice - and you've already taken your first step by opening this book. The skills you'll learn can be applied to work situations, family dilemmas, and other types of life challenges. It requires an all-in attitude in order to make a deep impact, and I'm excited to share my philosophy with you.

I want to spark a universe of possibilities by empowering you to act and create your own new positive reality.

To share your experiences and exchange feedback and ideas about Aggressive Positivity with me and others, join the conversation:

FACEBOOK

www.facebook.com/aggressivepositivity

INSTAGRAM

@aggressivepositivityofficial

Happy reading!

Limore

PS. Please note that this book is not intended as a substitute for professional help, medication, or treatment for those that suffer from serious depression or mental illness or other medical conditions.

HOW TO READ THIS BOOK

You can choose to read this book in the traditional way from start to finish, cover to cover, in pieces, or browse only those sections that interest you. If my journey/story/bio and personal anecdotes do not interest you, skip them and get to the practical and theoretical sections, or the opposite!

Some are inspired by hearing personal stories while others need a more mechanical/theoretical explanation. I have clearly labelled my personal stories/examples in bold Italics so that you can easily identify them and read them as you wish.

MY STORY

It all began long ago in 1977, when I was born as an incessantly screaming and excessively hairy baby. Through endless sleepless nights, my dad had to put me to sleep by singing and rocking me back and forth simultaneously. If he would stop singing or stop rocking, I would wail. They were hard but rewarding days for both my parents. My father says they were his favourite times. Lucky me - he still sings to me through happy and hard times, even through my tears.

I grew up in Thornhill, Ontario, Canada with my parents Betty (Batia) and John (Yochanan) Twena. My mom always taught me the value of thinking before speaking. The epitome of beauty, elegance, and class, she taught me to be honest, let go of my hang-ups and insecurities and to be fair and loyal to those I loved. My dad was always singing and dancing around, literally everywhere, bringing his special brand of joy to our household.

My brother, one year and a half year my junior, Allon, loved to cause trouble and together we were partners in crime. We spent days climbing trees, pulling pranks and laughing with one another. From him I learned how to be sensitive to others and to have fun despite any challenging circumstance.

Adi was born four years later and Allon finally had someone to pick on. Adi and I would spend our days singing in annoying voices, dressing up in ridiculous homemade costumes and talking about quantum mechanics. A born adventurer, he taught me to be curious about the world and explore it with courage.

Shira was born when I was seven, and our family was finally complete. Due to the age difference, I felt like Shira was simultaneously my sister and daughter. I was blessed with the opportunity to guide her through the challenges of growing up. Shira taught me to love with all my heart, accept myself and laugh about every possible body part!

My grandparents were the roots that kept the family united throughout various circumstances. My maternal grandparents, Hela and Henry Melnick, made a lasting impression on me. Surviving the Holocaust imbued them with a certain resiliency, tolerance, and strength that is difficult to describe.

In 2011, I chronicled and published Henry's survivorship experiences in a book titled "By My Mother's Hand" (if you are interested in reading it, you can find it on Amazon or www.bymymothershand.com). My grandfather married Elaine (Bubbie) after Hela's passing when I was 11 years old. Elaine's endless smiles and warmth filled my heart every time I saw her and I'm lucky to have her with me today. My grandparents served as a constant reminder to be grateful and the importance of perspective in life.

My paternal grandparents, Joseph and Pnina Twena, also made a deep impact on my worldview. My grandmother Pnina was diagnosed with Multiple Sclerosis (MS) at the young age of 39, and despite battling such a draining degenerative disease, she showed us the constant grit and humour that is necessary to enjoy life. She was brave in her struggle, especially during a time when MS treatments were not widely available. She spoke eleven (!) languages and had the singing voice of a nightingale in her youth.

My grandfather Joseph was always eager to hand out candies and little toys to the grandchildren, during religious festivals or otherwise. He placed a high importance on our cultural traditions growing up and beamed with pride as we recited prayers every holiday dinner surrounded by family. He served as a shining example of how to prioritize family over everything else.

Growing up, I was fortunate to have an amazing family, but I was not as fortunate with my social life. I was not popular at all in elementary school and spent most of my lunches crying in the bathroom. I was mostly made fun of f or my darker skin, "strange sounding" name and terrible fashion sense. But that turned around in high school, after my awkward braces came off. I met my best friend, a boyfriend and a loyal crew of girlfriends. I went on to perform in a local pop-opera band, school talent shows, fashion shows and played basketball. After high school, I pursued an undergrad business degree, after which I moved to Los Angeles to pursue music for three years. When I came home, I met the love of my life and finished an MBA.

I cycled through many different marketing-related jobs, and after giving birth to my three children, Gabriella, Eliana and Aviya, I was truly happy, and my heart had found its home.

Then, on Dec. 21st, 2016, I got the unexpected diagnosis that would change my life forever.

THE DIAGNOSIS

"You have breast cancer."

Those four words echoed through my body into the floor under my feet. A tsunami of panic, fear, shock, confusion, and disbelief clouded my mind. I could barely mouth the start of a question without first breaking down.

"But I'm a good person, why would G-d do this to me?" I asked the nurses. They looked at me and replied with a hint of humour, "honey, even bitches get cancer."

Although this didn't do much to comfort me at the time, I later admitted to myself that cancer is indiscriminate. I realized that it hits people of all races, colours, ages and religions. It hit you, if you were decent or cruel, considerate or selfish, mean or generous. The point was that it hit you - HARD. Over and over and over. It hit you at diagnosis. It hit you when you heard about the courses of treatment and the possible side effects. It hit you at home and it hit your family and friends.

The worst part? Having to look into my parents' and husbands' eyes that day. So much pain and worry lay ahead of us. It was by far, the single darkest moment of my life.

I cried for two days straight and the world genuinely cried along with me. I received calls, messages, and in-person visits. Despite their positive intentions, most of my well-wishers defaulted to grief and sadness. They were behaving as if I was already beaten. At that moment, I decided that I couldn't possibly go through this ordeal with so much weighing me down.

I made the conscious and deliberate decision to get through my illness like no one has ever seen. I was in a cloud of despair and uncertainty, yet I was determined to find a way through hell. To me, the only way through this was with positivity - the most aggressive type.

Following this, I instructed everyone around me to only talk about good things, including my doctors. Of course, I needed to hear the critical information, but I didn't want to hear about survival rates, recurrence rates, the full drug names and every single one of their potential side effects. I didn't want to talk about my illness - rather, I wanted to hear funny stories and laugh. I wanted to have fun and do anything and everything I ever dreamed of - and that was the start of my transformation.

This first moment when I consciously and deliberately changed my attitude and actions, was the beginning of the idea of Aggressive Positivity. It was this kind of behaviour that formed the basis of it all.

AGGRESSIVE POSITIVITY™ AN INTRODUCTION

After my breast cancer diagnosis, I heard a lot of well-intentioned sentiments such as, "I'm so sorry you have cancer. Be positive and you'll be OK."

How could I possibly be "positive" facing a gauntlet of chemotherapy, surgery, radiation, and endless tests? How could I be "positive" with the very real prospect of not being alive to be with my husband and watch my children grow?

Being "positive" didn't seem like a strong enough solution. I needed a way to overcome my prognosis that was powerful, "badass" and as intense as my challenge: AGGRESSIVE POSITIVITY sounded better. My thinking was that "You can't fight Darth Vader with a water gun - you need a sword. A white glowing sword, but a sword nonetheless!"

Below I will lay out a pared down version of the philosophy:

When you are slapped in the face with a challenge, you will most likely go through the expected phases of shock, denial, sadness and perhaps even anger. Everyone will cycle through these phases at their own pace, and that is OK. Take the time you need to properly digest and absorb the situation. After those initial phases comes acceptance.

Once you reach the phase of acceptance and are prepared to face your challenge, you are ready to begin deploying Aggressive Positivity and its three steps:

Step 1: Flip your mind

Step 2: Perform aggressive actions of love

Step 3: Deflect negativity

I will describe each step briefly below and will go into greater depth in the chapters ahead.

STEP 1: Flip Your Mind

First, you need to flip your mind. You need to take your negative thoughts and flip them into positive ones. For example, while going through treatment, I told myself that I'm not sick, I'm healing.

Still, your thoughts, like a pendulum, will go up and down. One moment you feel high, and the next your thoughts fall into the gutter. We can keep our thoughts high by following the next step.

STEP 2: Perform Aggressive Actions of Love

You must think of the activity that you love so much that it fuels you. Schedule that activity in such a way that you are consistently looking forward to something that gives you energy. In that way, your challenge fades in impact and importance, and you'll have the energy boost necessary to keep your thoughts positive.

STEP 3: Deflect Negativity

The last step is to deploy strategies to deflect negativity in your environment, the people around you and within yourself. Further along, I detail many strategies to support and help you achieve success in this area like recruiting an aggressively positive clan.

Getting Ready for Aggressive Positivity

Before attempting Aggressive Positivity, you need to acknowledge the challenge ahead of you and turn to face it. The acknowledgement process may take a few days, weeks, months, or even years, depending on your own situation. Whatever time you need, take it.

Give yourself permission to take your time and space to digest. Cry, scream, be angry, sad or scared. There are no rules here. Your reactions to your challenges are yours and yours alone. They are every bit as unique as your fingerprint.

Aggressive Positivity isn't about denying those feelings or being "happy" all the time. It is about realizing that it is possible to smile through a storm of tears, it is possible to smile after the storm and that behind those clouds the sun will shine down on you once again.

Your mind is your best weapon to bravely action a positive future. But that is easier said than done! Facing difficult situations can be so overwhelming that you freeze, retreat or shut down completely.

The Power of Laughter

Something that I found most helpful in facing my challenge was the power of laughter and choosing to have a sense of humour about my situation. I used this as a tool throughout my journey and the three steps of aggressive positivity. Laughter enabled and empowered me to face and overcome anything.

We've all heard it: laughter is the best medicine. Several notable studies have proven that laughing helps reduce anxiety[1], reduces blood pressure[2], boosts immunity[3] and acts as a natural antidepressant[4], especially to those undergoing medical treatment.

---

[1] Yovetich, N. A., Dale, J. A., & Hudak, M. A. (1990). Benefits of Humor in Reduction of Threat-Induced Anxiety. Psychological Reports, 66(1), 51–58.

[2] Moshtag Eshg, Zahra & Ezzati, Jaleh & Nasiri, Navideh & Ghafouri, Raziyeh. (2017). Effect of Humor Therapy on Blood Pressure of Patients Undergoing Hemodialysis. Journal of Research in Medical and Dental Science. 5. 10.24896/jrmds.20175615.

[3] Ryu, Shin, & Yang (2015). Effects of Laughter Therapy on Immune Responses in Postpartum Women. J Altern Complement Med. 2015 Dec;21(12):781-8.

We all have different sources of laughter - comedy shows, sports bloopers, funny home videos, or stand-up comic routines. Our ability to access comedic material has never been easier thanks to YouTube, Netflix and other on-demand video networks. Many fortunate people have a relative or friend that knows how to crack you up in an instant.

As with most concepts in this book, you need to choose to act and taking the time to laugh is no different. You can choose not to take yourself and life so seriously. You can choose to lighten it up! I encourage you to schedule time doing an activity that will result in giggling, chuckling, or belly laughing.

---

[4] Kim SH, Kook JR, Kwon M, Son MH, Ahn SD, Kim YH (2015). The effects of laughter therapy on mood state and self-esteem in cancer patients undergoing radiation therapy: a randomized controlled trial. J Altern Complement Med. 2015 Apr;21(4):217-22.

During my cancer treatment, I tried to take the time to watch reruns of Impractical Jokers (a hidden camera prank show). I watched every stand-up comedian on Netflix and went to live comedy shows. I also asked my friends to send me videos of their kids doing silly things. I relied heavily on laughter to reduce my stress and anxiety. At the same time, in order to maximize the positive effects of laughter, I refused to watch the news and went on a strict diet of movies that were either funny or uplifting. As a result, my mood improved, and my health followed.

Having a family member or friend accompany me to my hospital appointments always lightened the mood. They would help keep my mind off the upcoming tests or treatments and comforted me during the procedures. (There are many people that lack a good support network, and in the section "Recruiting Your Aggressively Positive Clan", I expand on how to build yourself a strong community.)

Throughout my journey there were many "serious" appointments that addressed surgery and treatment choices. They tended to be very sobering conversations, and I listened carefully to all the necessary details, but still had a hilarious time cracking jokes with the doctors and nurses in order to ease the burden.

(Let me preface the following stories with the fact that I do not endorse laughing at people or not taking doctor appointments seriously. I simply inserted humour in order to lighten the mood. Not everyone feels comfortable or is able to make funny jokes. I am sharing my experiences to demonstrate that there isn't "one way" to go through any particular situation. Feel free to carve your own way!)

Below are a few of the shenanigans that had a strong impact on the feeling of positivity in the room:

25

Chemo jokes

My chemotherapy treatments were long and drawn out, each session lasting about four hours. Most of the time I made small talk with my neighbours and it made the time go by faster.

During one of my treatments, there was a lady wearing a hijab sitting across from me. Naturally, we became friends after I sang her a song I knew in Arabic, and thereafter we felt comfortable chatting. I have no idea where this came from, but I asked her with a smirk, "Do you know what's good about being Muslim and having cancer?" A little shocked and confused, she replied, "What?" I then took my hands framing my forehead, covering what was left of my hair, and said "no one can tell!" We belly laughed so hard together about how she could choose who she wanted to tell about her illness because, as I had remarked, no one could tell she had lost her hair.

Losing hair

Another amusing moment came up during an appointment with my oncologist, shortly after my hair began to fall out from chemotherapy. I said to her, "When you said that my hair would fall out, I didn't realize that it would fall out everywhere (pointing 'down there')! I wish that it would stay that way from the neck down!" Laughter ensued and the appointment seemed easier to navigate, even though we were in the middle of a very sensitive conversation.

Nicest butt

Every month, I had to see a lovely nurse named Tamara to have medicine injected to shut down my ovaries. It was administered through the gluteus maximus, or in simple language, my butt. During one of my routine appointments, I hopped onto the examination chair face down, pulled down my jeans while anticipating the injection. I looked over my shoulder at Tamara and said, "Be honest, isn't this the most amazing butt you've seen all morning? "Of course, after chuckling, the needle that day hurt less than the others.

Dixarit

I had a wonderful obstetrician-gynaecologist surgeon Dr. Zaltz who, as a preventative measure, removed my ovaries post-treatment. As a result, I was instantly consumed by full-fledged menopausal symptoms, complete with hot flashes that woke me up at least six times a night. I was in Dr. Zaltz' office describing these symptoms when he said that he could prescribe "Dixarit," a common treatment. I immediately started howling from laughter with my mom. "Why are you laughing?" he asked, intrigued. I explained, "You don't see the humour in the fact that you are prescribing me DIX...R...IT?" (say it out loud) To which he replied, "I'm an OBGYN, if you were telling me a joke about vaginas, I'd get it, but talk about dicks and I'm lost." Again, you can imagine the laughter in the room.

Mo Hip

For those who know me, I have a million nicknames. From Limori to Lee Mo to Mo, Momo, MoJo, Moisha and Limo. In fact, people in my family hardly call me by my given name. I find this endearing and my most recent nickname also makes light of my situation. I love salsa dancing so Mo Hip became an easy moniker, and now that I only have one breast, I am Mo Hip One Tit! LOL. I am so thankful that I am not shy about my reality.

Ten Years Max

On my day of diagnosis, I felt depressed and decided to lie down as soon as I got home. My sister-in-law Sandy arrived to comfort me in bed. She surveyed the room, looked me in the eye, and said, "I'm giving you 10 years max." Confused and shocked, I replied, "What?" She continued, "You get ten years of my help with your cancer events, organizing speaking engagements, and other stuff. You're so annoying - you're going to go through this like a rock star and still be skinny and beautiful."

Of course, her well-intentioned sarcasm made me laugh through my tears. It reminded me of the importance of humour through desperate times.

Laughing while exercising

My Doctors recommended an hour of exercise daily to reduce the side effects of chemotherapy. I loved doing Zumba exercises by watching videos on YouTube in the comfort of my living room. One afternoon, I did my exercises with my sister Shira, who was egging me on to perform different ridiculous moves. Goofing off was and continues to be our normal way of behaving, and so this situation was no different. Being silly helped my motivation to move, because as you can imagine, I was in no mood to work out after treatments. But I pushed myself. The truth is that I was winded on the couch, after I finished filming my dance, but you can be sure that I was a hysterically giggly, wiped-out and happy lady.

You really have to see the video to understand the hilarity: (https://www.facebook.com/aggressivepositivity/videos/1944 157045799544?sfns=mo)

I hope that by now you have gotten to know me a little bit better, and maybe feel a little bit encouraged. This is because the funny moments that I just described happened during the hardest year and moments of my life. They happened on the day of diagnosis, during needles, and while getting chemo medicine through my veins. You can do this.

Now that you have reached acceptance with a little light heartedness on your side, let's dive into the individual steps of Aggressive Positivity:

STEP 1: FLIP YOUR MIND

In order to set the groundwork for effective mind flipping, you must separate the fact from the fiction in your head, because fiction will trigger your fears.

For instance, the fact is that tomorrow I need to give a speech in front of my peers. The fiction is that I will fail, and everyone will laugh at me or think less of me. Those fearful thoughts can prevent me from preparing and performing at my best. We all do this - we stress ourselves out of so many situations by focusing on what might happen, but we do not know the future.

The following strategy helped me calm my mind and in turn body, in preparation of flipping my mind.

Separating Fact from Fiction

A month before being diagnosed, I met a spiritual advisor Mira Leshem, while visiting Israel. My sister in-law spoke so highly of her that I insisted on going to one of her classes on the way to the airport! Back home in Canada, I continued to listen to her lectures through WhatsApp calls and 1 incorporated many of her teachings into my day-to-day life. She guided me through the turmoil of cancer.

One of the skills I learned from her was the power to overcome my tendency to automatically frame situations in a negative light. I took the facts of a situation and added negative "stories" around them that haunted my world. I didn't even notice this as an automatic behaviour. I was so deeply wired into my fears and previous negative experiences. Those fears tainted my thoughts about a future event with negativity, convincing my mind that everything will turn out badly.

Roy F. Baumeister, a prominent social psychologist and professor, explored this idea in a journal article he co-authored in 2001, "Bad Is Stronger Than Good," which appeared in The Review of General Psychology. He surmised that negative emotions require more cognitive energy to process, so they make more of an impact on our psyche than positive emotions.[5] I like to think of the concept like a plow in the field of brain cells, and the route more travelled forms a deeper groove.

For example, before a blood test, our mind defaults to negative associations such as fear and the pain of the needle. We spend hours, days or even weeks in anxious anticipation. Then, when the day arrives, we find ourselves surprised at how expertly the nurse inserts the needle, without feeling more than the tiniest pinch. Ultimately, we feel relieved at how relatively painlessly the test went over.

---

[5] Baumeister, Bratslavsky, Finkenauer, Vohs (2001). Bad Is Stronger Than Good. Review of General Psychology 2001. Vol. 5. No. 4. 323-370.

After realizing the needle was not THAT painful, you can understand how the energy and anxiety directed at the fear of the needle can be redirected.

It is far more efficient to live in the present moment. As we think about upcoming events, it's OK to consider all the possible outcomes, but make sure you are separating the facts from the fiction, within the stories you create in your mind.

Separating fact from fiction does not imply that you will never have moments of real fear or anxiety when facing tremendous challenges. This practice is simply trying to make you aware of what is real and what is just a possibility. You may not necessarily suffer but rather coast through various stages of your challenge, even surprising yourself!

Here are some examples of situations illustrating how you can separate fact from fiction:

FACT: I have a blood test tomorrow.

Fiction: The needle is going to hurt.

FACT: I have major surgery in three weeks.

Fiction: I will be out of commission and in pain for six weeks.

FACT: I had a major fight with my partner.

Fiction: Our relationship will never recover, and I have lost what we had.

You can easily imagine the fear and anxiety the fictions can induce!

I invite you to try this exercise. Think about an event or a situation that is worrying you. Think for a moment whether your worries are rooted in the "stories" and future visions that may or may not come true. Remember that you can only control what is within your ability to control.

Use this space to jot down some of your own situations and try to separate your fact vs. fiction.

FACT:

FICTION:

FACT:

FICTION:

FACT:

FICTION:

Performing Mind Flips

Now that you have separated fact from fiction in your head, you are ready to perform mind flips.

Regardless of how dark or intimidating a specific situation may seem, you can always choose to "flip" your outlook. In fact, the more extreme and challenging the situation is, the easier it is to think of the flipped desired state of mind. For example, a hateful situation can become loving, hot to cold, sickness to health.

This is difficult at the start, but with practice it becomes second nature. If you can separate facts from fiction in your situation, as discussed above, then you will have an easier time mind flipping.

It takes effort and conscious intention to flip to the good. There are endless beautiful, charitable, touching, and warm moments that happen every second of every day - yet somehow, they don't capture our attention. Our default mindset is to focus on the negative, since it is the easier way to think. Thus, we must work against our nature to think of the positive. Yes, I said work, this is going to take much effort.

A good place to try mind flipping is during an ordinary day. For me, a typical day consists of a never-ending stream of appointments, activities, emails, piles, chores, crumbs, demanding job situations and long list of things to do to take care of my three children. Below I describe an everyday moment that I flipped for the better.

Personal Story: Drumming Out the Door

One moment that used to set me up for failure for the rest of the day, was the simple act of leaving the house on a weekday morning. Getting my kids to the door for school used to include a frantic screaming me, trying to move children and their school backpacks to the car. Of course, I was all hyped-up, raising my voice, yelling the familiar "we're gonna be late!", while their speed resembled waiting for salt to thaw an iceberg. I always ended up feeling stressed out and tired after the ordeal, and I needed a change. So, I flipped it - I decided that I am no longer rushing children out the door - we were going to dance instead. Stressful rushing flipped to dancing.

The next morning, I explained to my kids that when they hear me drumming a beat on the wall, they are supposed to dance towards the door. So, I went to the wall and banged out a very rudimentary beat, with a guttural "huh" on the tail end, to help the beat along. I then demonstrated a weird goofy dance to the door. Of course, loving this new game, my kids played along and walked with rhythm to the door. This new way of leaving the house helped my mood for the rest of the day. Of course, this didn't mean that I didn't have setbacks, tantrums, and hard moments in the morning anymore, however, in general, we had a more positive experience leaving the house.

Performing mind flips requires razor sharp focus on the positive within each challenge. The first opportunity I had to perform a major life mind flip came shortly after acceptance of my cancer diagnosis. I quickly exclaimed, "I'm not sick, I am healing." I told myself that statement repeatedly, every single day. "I'm not sick, I'm healing. I'm healing, I'm healing." I later expanded that, "I'm healthier now than I was yesterday, even if the treatments make me feel lousy."

Mind flips aren't easy to embrace, at least at the start. Some might seem far-fetched or even silly. But if you repeat them and truly believe in your power to change your state of mind, they accumulate and begin to have a profound effect on your overall positivity. **What matters most is our interpretation of our situation, rather than the circumstance itself.**

To help perform mind flips, try talking through situations with family and friends. Another strategy is to seek out someone who is going through a similar challenge - for example, two new parents can help each other sympathize, find the humour, and even the positive aspects of performing midnight diaper duty.

If I was able to apply mind flips to the horrid process of going through cancer treatment, imagine other everyday challenges that can be flipped. Adversity can expose opportunities - it all depends on your mindset.

As Albert Einstein famously said, **"The most important decision we make is whether we believe we live in a friendly or hostile universe."**

A good place to start is by thinking of the exact opposite word to whatever you are going through: for example:

sick >< healing,

financial trouble >< abundance

war >< peace

isolation >< connection

Then think of a way to reframe the situation.

Below are some mind flips that helped begin my aggressively positive state of mind:

- ☐ I'm not sick, I am healing.
- ☐ It's not chemotherapy, it's medicine.
- ☐ It's not surgery, the doctors are saving my life.

I encourage you to use this space to jot down your own mind flips.

CHALLENGE:

FLIP:

CHALLENGE:

FLIP:

CHALLENGE:

FLIP:

Mind Flip Examples

I am aware that not everyone has the mind frame, energy or tools necessary to mind flip situations on their own. Some may feel stuck and unable to think because of high levels of stress and pure exhaustion from different life circumstances. Some are genetically more predisposed to being positive than others. Still, some may lack the experience or are scared to try.

It is for this reason that I created a mind flip list for different situations or challenges and thoughts that I have experienced personally or watched others overcome.

This is by no means an exhaustive list and can't possibly cover every challenging situation a human may face, but it can be a source of inspiration and help jumpstart the process for you:

School & Work

- I am not being tested, I am being challenged to learn.

- I am not unemployed, I am now free to choose my path.

- I am not making money in destructive ways, I am earning a living through productive and endless partnerships.

- I am not broke, I am humbly prosperous and full of blessings.

- My co-worker is not trying to knock me down, she is challenging me to perform at my best.

Environment

- It is not dirty in here, I have a chance to organize and create my environment to my liking.

- We are not in conflict, we will actively work to diminish our points of disagreement and chase areas of agreement.

- We are not at war, we are seeking peace within ourselves.

- I'm not in hell, I chose to create heaven wherever I am.

Health

- I'm not sick, I'm healing.

- It's not chemo, it's medicine.

- It's not surgery, they're saving my life.

- I'm not infertile, I am filled with endless powers of creation.

Friendship and Relationships

- We didn't fight, we have gained a deeper understanding of each other's needs.

- I am not in conflict; I will reach out in friendship.

- He didn't break up with me; I'm now free to pursue true love.

- I am not drawn to negative people and relationships; I choose to surround myself with generous souls whenever I can.

- I'm not lonely, I attract deep rich relationships.

- I am not impotent, I share love, affection, and passion with my partner to light up their world.

- I don't feel unloved, I chose to love myself and all those around me with all they are going through.

- I don't have trouble receiving love, I realize that by receiving I can then share that love with myself and others.

Personal Growth

- I didn't make mistakes in my past, I learn from my experiences so that I can live happily in the present moment.

- I'm not tired and tapped out of energy, I have time to focus on what I need to recharge.

- I don't feel envious, I will focus on making miracles in my own world.

- I do not have destructive thoughts, I am allowing my thoughts to run free for a bit so that the good thoughts have room to come in.

- I am not lost, I am discovering my purpose.

- I'm not stressed, I'm dissolving negative energy.

- I'm not surrounded by negative people, I am encouraging support by positive souls in my life.

- I am not short sighted, I look to the future with the end result in mind.

- I am not depressed, I am blessed with the strength to stand up after falling with the faith and determination that I can.

- It's not all about me and my journey, I enjoy the collective achievements and fulfilment of purpose, of my family and community.

- I don't keep to myself, I share my deep wisdom with those around me so that I can uplift.

- I am not jealous, I take responsibility for my thoughts and actions.

- I'm not lying, I have the courage to listen and speak.

- My life is not a mess, I have the power to structure my life for peace and happiness.

- I don't hate, I forgive all for their faults, including my own.

- I am not a quitter, I have the grit to see my projects through.

- I don't forget, I am blessed with the power to learn and apply deep lessons from my past.

- I am not negative, I recognize the dark thoughts within me thereby setting them free to leave.

- I am not stubborn, I free myself from my ego and choose to see another way.

- I am not afraid, I fearlessly face my challenges and separate facts and the truth from stories I created in my head.

- I am not petty, I see the opportunity to learn from every little moment in my life.

- Life is not raining on me, I know how to dance in the storm creating my own narrative with my mind.

- I don't gossip, I use my words to uplift my universe.

- I am not a victim of my circumstances, I have the power of perspective.

- I do not hesitate, I trust myself with full confidence to make the best decisions that I can.

- I'm not selfish, I can empathize with those around me and am open to seeing things differently.

- I'm not sad, I let go of my past mistakes so that I can live happily in the present moment.

- I don't feel guilty, I make no apologies for my faults and definitely not for my strengths!

- I do not have an ulterior motive, I give because I enjoy the friendships and joy that come from pure love.

- I don't ignore what my soul is telling me, I feel deeply about what my next step should be and bravely move ahead.

- I'm not hopeless, I reach out for help to rise above darkness.

- I am not unbalanced, I strive to grow with each experience.

- I am not a preacher, I humbly share wisdom with love.

- I do not take things for granted, I appreciate every small and large blessing and especially appreciate the people around me.

- I am not down on myself, I am confident in the most beautiful parts of my soul that radiates.

- I am not invisible, everyone around me can feel my strong presence.

- I do not hate, I recognize the common humanity within all of us.

- I do not judge, I only judge myself confident that I did my best within my power at that moment.

- I am not a victim, I have the power to make decisions that will change my circumstances.

- I have no expectations, I am what I am at this moment.

- I do not doubt, I know there is a long-term plan for me and everyone else.

Ahead I share some personal stories with you that illustrate how I used mind flips during my cancer treatment journey. I hope that my ideas spark a light within you and give you the courage to flip too!

Living My Journey in Public

For the first few weeks following the loss of my hair, I wore a wig in public as most cancer patients do. I was digesting the fact that I no longer had hair, it was February, the Canadian winter was unforgiving, and I hadn't yet considered any other option. I wore a wig made of my own hair, but I still didn't feel like myself. I felt uncomfortable because the wig pressed on my head and gave me headaches. I also felt like I was hiding something - my baldness, my disease, my pain, my weakness, and my strength. I didn't want to hide my illness from the world, and I felt the need to share it so that I could gather strength from my family, friends, and community.

So, I flipped the feeling of hiding into living my truth out in public (here you can identify the flip-able terms hiding><public).

About a month and a half into my treatments, I was scheduled to sing at an all-women charity event that was raising money for a local food bank. On the day of my performance, I took up a friend's generous offer to do my makeup. Liraz expertly applied makeup to hide my barely visible eyelashes and eyebrows. I felt beautiful. Gorgeous. Bald.

After getting home, I dressed up in a lovely cocktail dress and donned an amazing looking Cleopatra-style wig. I also cut up one of my girls velvet leggings, into a cool looking armband, to cover up my PICC line (a semi-permanent Intravenous directly to the heart that I needed for 4 months, because Chemo was damaging to my veins).

At the gala, I sang a few songs before sharing with the audience that I am going through a very challenging time and proceeded to tell them my story. After sharing from my heart, I instantly felt more liberated and greatly relieved. My wig had been itching me the whole night, gently yet consistently squeezing my head to the point where it was almost unbearable. I figured the audience was now aware of my condition, so I said, "I hope you don't mind if I take this off."

No sooner had I peeled the wig off my head, 400 women roared to their feet in support. Clapping, screaming, and crying, these women showed me how much they cared, loved, and supported me! I was moved beyond words.

After the crowd settled, I sang my newly minted song "Alive," written two days after my first chemo treatment.

That night, I changed my Facebook profile photo from my old long-haired self to a beautiful bald selfie. That night was the night I consciously decided to live out my journey in public, in the open, and bald.

You can imagine the public outpouring of love and support I received that night, both from those at the performance and from social media. The support and encouragement did wonders for my state of mind and confidence. I could proudly walk around as myself in what felt like the most authentic me.

To watch me take off my wig, type "Limore takes off wig" into YouTube or type the following link in your browser:

https://youtu.be/I8SLKMSyXXI

Sheep Shearing Day

I have had beautiful, long, thick hair my whole life. As a side effect of my upcoming chemo treatments, I faced the inevitability of losing it all. The biggest challenge was communicating this to my three kids. How could I make this situation less traumatic and dare I say - gasp - fun?

First off, to make the transition to baldness less extreme for all of us, I cut my hair very short. My kids had a fun time teasing me for looking like a boy. Then I had an idea. I started showing the kids real videos of farmers shearing their sheep. They eventually started questioning "Mummy, why are you showing us these videos of farmers shearing sheep?" to which I replied, "because you're each going to get a turn doing that to mummy on Sheep Shearing Day!"

You can only imagine the intrigue and excitement at the prospect of getting a turn at shaving my head!

For the next two weeks, my kids woke up every morning squealing, "Is it sheep shearing day today? Is it sheep shearing day today?" They loved to argue over who would be first and what kind of haircut they would give me.

One afternoon, I grabbed a bunch of hair in my hand and gave it a good tug. The entire clump came right out. Finally, Sheep Shearing Day had arrived. I announced the big news with excitement. My husband, kids, and I gathered in our master washroom. My siblings came over to add to the fun! We all took turns climbing into the tub, with reggaeton music blasting in the background, and everyone had a turn shaving parts of my head. We danced and laughed and made mohawk designs in my hair. It was an experience my family will always remember.

Now it is important to note that my children were very young at the time - my eldest was seven and youngest was three, and they had no idea how potentially devastating, painful, and traumatic it could be for me to lose my hair. All they remember is Sheep Shearing Day.

I also want to acknowledge that even though we laughed throughout that night, the adults who understood were also sad because the loss of my hair was now a visual reminder of my illness. **Aggressive Positivity is not about glossing over difficult realities - it is about making them better.**

What I am saying is that it is OK to cry. However, I am also saying that it is possible to laugh through those hard times! I flipped losing my hair to Sheep Shearing Day.

Making CAT Scans FUN Scans

As part of a complete diagnosis, I had to have a standard full body CAT scan to determine whether my cancer had spread to anywhere other than the breast and lymph nodes. It was quite a frightening time due to all the unknowns.

My husband Isaac accompanied me to that CAT scan appointment. He waited with great anticipation and anxiety as I walked away from him into the preparation room.

Here was my chance to separate fact from fiction.

FACT: I have a CAT scan today

FICTION: It will be terrible, scary, and sad.

It was also an opportunity to perform a mind flip - could a CAT scan become a FUN scan, I wondered?

In the preparation room, I saw seven elderly men awaiting their turn. Everyone had their own hospital bed but without a barrier or separating drapes. It felt like we were all in it together.

The nurse approached me and asked which arm I'd prefer to have the IV inserted and I instinctively raised my right arm. Only after insertion of the IV, did I realize that I just immobilized my right arm for what may be a long waiting time. A bit frantic, I asked the nurse, "Hey, can I still text with my right hand?" Immediate laughter followed from my seven new CAT scan buddies and hospital staff. The nurse responded, "In my life I have never had a patient ask if they can text during a CAT scan." I was happy that I was able to liven up the mood, in an otherwise sombre setting.

The nurse went on to explain that during the scan, dye would be injected into my arm, which may cause me to feel hot. The heat would likely start from my neck and move downwards, intensifying "down there" (the nurses' words, not mine). The conversation was easily overheard, so, of course, all eyes in the room were on me as I repeated her words with a smirk, "It'll get hot down there." Again, the room erupted in laughter.

My name was called to enter the scanning room shortly thereafter. Already giddy from the earlier laughs, I recognized one of the scanning technicians as being Polish by his name. I began to sing him a song my grandmother taught me in Polish. He started laughing, explaining that he hadn't heard that song since his grandmother was alive. I was happy to bring a smile to his face.

I then jumped onto the scanning table, laughed with the technicians and exclaimed, "Alright guys, I'm ready to have some fun!" They explained the routine technical details about the machine, about the dye injection feeling hot and what to expect and left the room.

I was amused as this deep voice, seemingly out of nowhere, said "breathe," and the machine propelled me in and out of a donut-shaped scanner. The voice continued to instruct me to either hold my breath or breathe, during which the dye flowed through my veins. Indeed, this created a very amazingly hot sensation, especially "down there." As you can imagine, my thoughts drifted back to my smiling companions in the waiting room as I thought to myself, "this was way more fun than I could ever have hoped!"

After my IV was taken out, I walked back to the waiting room to find Isaac slumped over his chair, looking sad. He had spent the last hour imagining my torture, pain, fear, and anxiety due to the scan. He looked up at me and asked "So, how was it?" I looked at him and replied, with pep in my voice, "It was fun!" He looked at me, perplexed. "What? What do you mean?" he mumbled, clearly confused. I proceeded to recount my little adventure back to him. Shaking his head, he said, "Only you! I'm sitting here worrying like crazy and you're having fun. "

And that, my friends, is how I turned a CAT scan into a FUN scan.

STEP 2: PERFORM AGGRESSIVE ACTIONS OF LOVE

This is the second and most important step to Aggressive Positivity: performing **Aggressive Actions of Love**. You must support your newly flipped positive state of mind with actions that give you an abundance of energy, or you risk your hard-mental work not sticking. Why? Because our thoughts are fleeting.

As mentioned earlier, our thoughts go up and down like a pendulum, and just as easily as you were on a high, a split second later you can find yourself on a low. How do you minimize the inevitable downward swing in positivity?

You must perform actions. Not just any kind of actions - we are fighting demons here! We need aggressive actions of love. What does that mean? It means you have to find the activity (or activities) that you love so much that it fills you with positive energy and then schedule it aggressively, meaning as often as humanly possible.

The action can be anything from going for a walk with your dog, reading a book, or singing karaoke using a YouTube video. You can visit a friend, exercise, or cook a food you were craving. Thankfully we live in a virtual world, where you can access almost anything online. Want to learn guitar? How about taking a course in logic, the art of negotiation or astronomy? There are universities, podcasts and various organizations that offer endless possibilities. Whatever it is, you need to schedule that activity **aggressively** so that you are constantly looking forward to it. Performing that action will fuel you and your challenge will seem to fade in impact and importance. In addition, the energy generated by that action is what will give you the power to fight back your negative thoughts.

Why the word "Aggressive"? Because we are facing an aggressive challenge here! Without the strong momentum of energy that aggressivity brings, the accompanying positivity would fall flat. Conversely, brute force without a purpose is aimless. Only a combination of positivity and aggressiveness will achieve results. **Remember how aggressively your challenge hit you - you need to hit back harder.**

It is important to note that the action needs to be large in its impact on you, not necessarily in magnitude of the action itself. In other words, a walk in the park with your niece may provide you with as much energy as a painting class or concert may provide another person. The important part is that you are getting filled up with energy. It is especially difficult to flip your mind when you are in a stressful situation with low energy, making it even more important to take aggressive action as soon as possible!

If you don't have a passion, hobby, or "thing" that fills you up, it's never too late to find one! The criteria are simple. How good do you feel after said activity? Do you feel light? Energized? Happy? Invigorated? Inspired? If so, then you are probably on the right track. Keep trying different things until you find your own Action of Love.

The frequency of this activity is completely individual, whether it is scheduled every day, week, month, or quarter. What matters is that it is scheduled often enough to give you the fuel you need to move forward with your flipped state of mind.

Performing such mental and physical acrobatics seems like magic, and in the following sections I will dive deeper into how to ensure you have a better chance of success. You will benefit   from:

a) Finding, chasing and scheduling your Action of Love

b) Recruiting your Aggressively Positive Clan to support you

c) Releasing yourself from healing others

d) Releasing others from the responsibility of healing you

e) Forgiving yourself and others and releasing anger

f) Exercising your body and mind

g) Feeding the soul through meditation and/or prayer

h) Creating an aggressively positive physical environment

a) Find, Chase and Schedule What You Love

Expanding further on the concept of Aggressive Actions of Love, it is critical to find what moves you. We live in a society that is always go-go-go, and rarely do we find the time to sit and reflect on what actually makes us happy and fulfilled. We "fill" all our moments with activities, work, and devices.

When you find yourself in a miserable cycle, you can't see the future as easily because you - subconsciously or otherwise - do not want to see the future. Who would want to envision their future life in a job they hate, or in a relationship that is counter-productive? No one. That is why you do not seem to progress as quickly in a job you despise and seem to thrive within a work environment that is positive. Of course, many of you are in specific work situations that you cannot control, but there are many aspects of your life that you can control as mentioned above, and at minimum you can control your perspective.

The idea here is that you are choosing to affect your future. You are actioning a more positive future, thereby affecting how you feel in the present. You will feel that you have more energy and control over your life if you are getting consistent energy boosts from your activities. It will literally spark your next move!

My personal Aggressive Action of Love (beyond spending time with my family and friends) is singing. Below you can read about my love of music and how I used it to uplift, energize and heal myself.

Healing Through Music

Whether he is blasting Eydie Gorme y Los Panchos, Latin Summer Hits, or Rock n' Roll from the sixties, my dad John is always listening to music. When he is in the office, his car, working out, or just hanging out in the backyard, music follows his every step. He embodies his own philosophy or Johnnyism that "music makes you happier."

It's obvious to see that music brings him joy, and now the science exists to prove this phenomenon. In one study, music interventions showed beneficial effects on anxiety, pain, mood, and quality of life in patients diagnosed with cancer.[6] In another, patients with coronary heart disease saw benefits to their anxiety levels from music therapy.[7]

I definitely inherited my father's love of singing, dancing and listening to music whenever possible. This love of music has accompanied me throughout my life's challenges and celebrations. Music provided me an escape both physically and mentally and was and always will be a lifelong ally by my side.

During my challenging year, I was determined to use my love of music to make myself happy in order to speed up my healing. One of the first questions I asked my oncologist after

---

[6] Bradt J., Dileo C., Grocke D., Magill L. (2011). Music interventions for improving psychological and physical outcomes in cancer patients. Cochrane Database Syst Rev. 2011 Aug 10;(8):CD006911.

[7] Bradt, J., Dileo, C., & Potvin, N. (2013). Music for stress and anxiety reduction in coronary heart disease patients. Cochrane Database of Systematic Reviews, 12, CD006577.

my breast cancer diagnosis was whether the treatments will affect my voice. She told me that the treatments should not have an impact on my ability to sing. At that very moment, I excitedly turned to my husband and exclaimed, "I'm recording an album!"

Two days after my first treatment, I penned my first song of the album titled "Alive." I enlisted the help of my family member, Kayla Diamond, to help me write and record the song. We wrote it together in an hour and a week later recorded it in the studio with my sister Shira singing backup vocals with Kayla. Michael Nissim graciously offered to create the idea, film and edit the video for Alive two months later, while I was still undergoing chemo.

Search "Limore Alive" on YouTube to see the video or enter the link below in your browser:

https://youtu.be/cl4sqL5IKmI

I found the creative experience so energizing and uplifting that I decided to follow a methodical timetable of writing a song one week, then recording it the next. Kayla selflessly gave of her time and energy to make my dream come true.

Of course, there were long breaks throughout the process due to surgeries and treatment complications, but those writing and recording dates kept me excited and motivated through many very unpleasant medical experiences. I would let my nurses, doctors, and surrounding patients in the waiting rooms hear my latest song idea and it changed the mood in all of us.

I would obsessively analyse the production of the songs, each instrument, volume levels, vocal expressions and adlibs. Most days, driving to the hospital with my dad, we would be listening to a new song in various stages of creation. I would share the song with my friends and family and took in all their feedback. This had such a powerful impact on the conversations that occurred between us! I was engrossed in talking about my music instead of my condition, current state, medication, or treatment.

I found myself scheduling my most exciting recording sessions and performances right before or after my most difficult procedures on purpose. The contrast between the two activities was shocking at times. The day before my mastectomy and lymph node removal surgery, I spent a few hours recording the second last song on the album, "Thank You." Those four hours were like an intense therapy session - all I was able to think about was the music. I kept reviewing my lyrics, delivery, emotions and notes.

Of course, the anxiety and stress of the upcoming surgery came back right after leaving the studio, but the imprint of negative thoughts on my mind was greatly lessened because my focus was on my Aggressive Action of Love and the energy it gave my body. I was not only distracted for a few hours, I was *floating*. I felt literally on a high, because I was engaged in an activity that filled me up to the core. Imagine what that does to your body and immune systems' ability to heal? Instead of spending the entire day anxious for the surgery, which would be typical and understandable, I only spent half the day in that state.

In another Aggressive Action of Love, I performed onstage at a local festival four days after that same surgery. Still on strong painkillers, with my drains hidden behind my back under a jacket, I sang my heart out. That scheduled performance was my motivation to get out of bed. I was instructed by my doctor that I should not be lying down all day long and try walking around for ten minutes a few times a day. I figured that I could sing for a few minutes and then sit down! To see that performance, go to my Instagram account @limoremusic and search June 4th, 2017 or type the following link in your browser:

https://www.instagram.com/p/BU7_ZgNDvRg/

The dedication to singing went on for the duration of my treatments, until I fulfilled my dream of a complete album of six songs. It was truly magical!

To hear my full album, search "Limore Alive" on iTunes or Spotify.

I continue to use music to keep me healthy. In the Media section in the Appendix, you can explore links to my musical adventures, which include a few viral videos, my album, blog articles, international TV appearances, a mini documentary, and a full concert in Toronto that raised $15K for 3 different cancer related charities!

b) Recruit Your Aggressively Positive Clan

"If you support each other as family (either blood or chosen), no one will ever be left behind."

My mom and dad taught us this valuable lesson while we were growing up, mostly through their actions but also through their words. I have vivid memories of my mother shopping for organic carrots and juicing them for my grandmother as she was suffering through ovarian cancer. My mother always reminded my siblings and I through our fights, "When I'm gone, you will only have each other."

Throughout my childhood, I watched as my dad selflessly cared for his wheelchair-bound mother. He drove us to her apartment for visits several times a week and took us all on fun weekend adventures to help her endure a difficult and drawn out disease (multiple sclerosis) with humour and hope.

My grandmother always said that we (the grandchildren) were her reason for living. She had framed 8x10 blown up photos of each of her grandchildren's faces lined up opposite her bed, so that we would be the first thing she would see every morning, when she would open her eyes. For my Safta (grandmother) Pnina, spending time with her grandchildren was her Aggressive Action of Love.

My husband and kids, both of my parents, siblings, in-laws (mother, father, sisters, and brothers-in-law), extended family, and friends accompanied me through my challenging year and I can confidently say that it made a huge impact on my mental well-being. Whether accompanying me to appointments, or providing a well needed distraction, laugh or supporting my husband and children, they were there when I needed them most. I learned to say what I needed and ask for help from those around me. In contrast, prior to my illness, I belittled my needs for fear of being too needy or a bother to others. Sometimes I felt that my needs were not justified or real or important. I just wanted to make everyone happy, while sacrificing my own happiness. Sound familiar?

I learned through my hard experience that having a strong family unit (both blood and chosen) was extremely beneficial in navigating my ups and downs. I had a perpetual feeling that

I was safe, that someone who cared was watching out for my well-being. That feeling was both empowering and invigorating.

What I am saying about family and the benefits of having a strong support group around you is corroborated by science. Prolonged and deep loneliness can often lead to diseases of the body and mind. In fact, a recent study demonstrated that feelings of loneliness led to higher biomarkers of inflammation and reduced activity of anti-viral genes. People that reported feeling lonely also had increased activity of the sympathetic nervous system, the part of the nervous system responsible for the fight-or-flight response to stress or threats[8].

This highlights the importance of recruiting or creating an Aggressively Positive clan and their role in providing support.

[8] Myeloid differentiation in social isolation

Steven W. Cole, John P. Capitanio, Katie Chun, Jesusa M. G. Arevalo, Jeffrey Ma, John T. Cacioppo

Proceedings of the National Academy of Sciences Dec 2015, 112 (49) 15142-15147; DOI: 10.1073/pnas.1514249112

While enduring a life challenge, close family and friends tend to amplify their support.

Not everyone has a built-in support system within their family structure. Some lack a support network entirely! Some have moved away to new countries in search of better lives. Others have broken homes or unfortunate circumstances. Others still have families that are dysfunctional.

In these cases, feel empowered to create and choose a clan of your own. Consider the action of recruiting your clan with the objective of being Aggressively Positive! There are many resources out there to help you, you just need to be brave enough to reach out. Some ideas and sources I came across are below:

- Local Church, Synagogues, Mosques and other religious institutions usually have various support groups or religious clergy able to provide various levels of support

- Local Community Centre/Gym and Yoga studios

- Hospital programs: my hospital had many organized groups that offered a wide variety of help, which included volunteers that would come to your chemo appointments

- Social Media Groups: search for whatever challenge you have on Facebook or Instagram and you will have an endless supply of challenge-specific support groups, for example: Moms with twins forum, Leukaemia Survivors Group, Alcoholic Anonymous Toronto, etc.

- Workplace support groups or hotlines: many workplaces offer various support groups or even hotlines to support mental health

- Friend circles: reaching out to even one friend that has been through what you are experiencing and has come out on top is a great way to inject hope in a seemingly dismal prognosis. Having a friend that is positive, funny, or a great listener is priceless. Friends are magical.

If you can, I recommend trying to find a group that meets in person. The human-to-human interaction boosts all kinds of feel-good chemicals, alleviates loneliness, and makes us happier. We are meant to be social beings. It doesn't matter if the interactions are on a more intimate one-on-one basis or in a group at a cafe. The key is to have actual and real interactions with others. However, if that is not possible, Facetime and Zoom offer easy ways to interact digitally that will boost your feelings of connectivity.

Don't be afraid to reach out but be selective - you are seeking positive energy from good people. Also, it is helpful to communicate your expectations of support. For me, that meant explicitly communicating my desire to "only hear good things," and I avoided most conversations about my actual condition and progress.

Obviously, during times of need, there are situations we cannot control, and we cannot be 100% selective about who keeps our company. In these cases, we can redirect aggressive negativity, more on this later. In addition, some people have a different approach to dealing with challenges and feel compelled to share every detail of their medical condition as a form of venting and offloading. Whatever makes you feel better, is the right thing for you. The bottom line is that it is good for your wellbeing to have the support you need, in the way that you need it.

Similar to the approach of scheduling your activity of love as described earlier, find a mutual time to regularly schedule social time with your clan so that you feel happy, fulfilled and supported.

I began recruiting those around me to get in on the "Aggressive Positivity" approach as early on as diagnosis. I told my doctors and anyone I interacted with to only talk about positive things while I deflected unnecessary conversations about my condition, treatments, or prognosis. I never heard anything about survival rates, recurrence rates related to my illness, or even what stage I was - this was my choice.

In response to my requests, friends and family started sending me a barrage of funny videos, pictures, clips and telling me about embarrassing and hilarious situations to lift my spirits. If you know anything about my family, you know that we appreciate the value of a fart joke.

The support from my clan continued throughout treatment and I couldn't have gone through my journey as smoothly and happily as I did without them.

c) Release Yourself from Healing Others

As part of a healthy relationship, we all find ourselves consoling, advising, and helping those around us get through their daily ups and downs of life, as well as the larger obstacles that invariably come up. The quandary here is that when you are in the throes of an aggressive challenge yourself, you need every ounce of your energy and time to dedicate to yourself. For me, it was a matter of life and death.

My medical prognosis was so serious that it took all my energy to pull myself out of the well. I had to have some difficult conversations with those closest to me. I told them that I had to release myself from the duty of healing them from their everyday challenges, so that I could focus all my energy on healing myself.

The sobering conversations sounded something like this: "I love you so much. I am so sorry, but I can't be there for you for this short period of time, because I need every ounce of my being focused on healing my body and my life." Of course, everyone was very understanding, and it also allowed them to lend some of their energy to my healing as well. Releasing myself from supporting and uplifting others (other than my kids, of course) was one of the more liberating moments of my journey.

Remember that the life challenge you're going through is temporary, so this is not a permanent situation. Having the conversation with those you tend to support can be awkward, but it is extremely healing to release yourself from this commitment and frees up an unexpectedly large amount of energy and time that will be refocused on you!

d) Release Others From Healing You

Another helpful exercise in alleviating the stress and pain around life challenges is **releasing others of the responsibility of healing you**. With their helpful advice, guidance, and support, our spouses, partners, family members, and friends spend an enormous amount of energy and time "fixing" and "healing" us from our troubles. This is an extremely heavy load and, you are the only one that can fix you. You need to take responsibility for healing yourself! Ultimately you are the one that needs to act on their advice.

You may or may not decide to have a conversation to release those you perceive take responsibility for fixing you. I did have that conversation and it was yet another difficult moment. It went something like this: "I know you think that you have been fixing me all of these years, but the truth is that I am the only one that can fix me and the only one that can pull myself out of this situation. So, I am releasing you from the duty of fixing me, but I'm also releasing myself from fixing you for now."

Ouch. It was so painful to say those words. But it was necessary for my survival and to help those around me be light and supportive rather than sink with the heaviness of responsibility.

e) Forgive and Release Others

It's very natural for all of us to hold onto anger from time to time. You know the feeling - that twinge in your heart that you carry around after you feel wronged. The pain could emerge from something innocuous, like a simple accident, or something deeper like a betrayal from a partner.

My dad John believes that holding onto anger literally makes you sick - period. His Hebrew expression "Ee mecheela mevee machala" means "Being unforgiving brings disease" is so critical in a tumultuous time.

The source, depth, or intensity of the anger is unimportant. Even the concept of who is right and wrong is irrelevant. The point is that you are holding onto anger and resentment inside of your body, which can have a significant impact on your health.

Obviously, there are situations where a healthy dose of anger is not only appropriate, but necessary. Oftentimes, anger can spur us into action and force us to grow. However, if it lingers too long and festers unresolved, it can harm both our long and short term physical and mental well-being.

In fact, several studies, including one published in Psychosomatic Medicine, showed how suppressed anger demonstrated a strong correlation with the likelihood of having hypertension[9].

Yet another study found that emotional arousal had a profound impact on blood pressure - those that reported themselves as feeling happy had significantly lower blood pressure than those that said they were anxious or angry[10].

[9] Dimsdale, J. E., Pierce, C., Schoenfeld, D., Brown, A., Zusman, R., & Graham, R. (1986). Suppressed anger and blood pressure: The effects of race, sex, social class, obesity, and age. Psychosomatic Medicine, 48(6), 430–436. https://doi.org/10.1097/00006842-198607000-00005

[10] James, G. D., Yee, L. S., Harshfield, G. A., Blank, S. G., & Pickering, T. G. (1986).

That is why we must forgive, learn and move on. The first part is being aware of the anger, the next and more difficult step is forgiving and letting go - your health depends on it. **You can mind flip your memories of the past!**

I used to hold onto a lot of anger against those I perceived had hurt me, whether it was a friend, an ex-boyfriend, ex-boss, or a colleague. I would perpetuate my pain by holding on to the situation and talking about it, rather than striving to take a step back and trying to see the positive that emerged from the situation.

Over time, I accumulated a mountain-sized amount of pain that I carried with me in my body and mind. My pain weighed heavily on my heart and when I got ill, I no longer had room for the negativity that came with recalling the past.

The influence of happiness, anger, and anxiety on the blood pressure of borderline hypertensives. Psychosomatic Medicine, 48(7), 502–508. https://doi.org/10.1097/00006842-198609000-00005

There and then, I decided to release and forgive anyone and everyone for everything. I wrote an extensive list of all the people that I felt had hurt me. I surprised myself at how long my list was, and I cannot overstate how therapeutic this exercise became. I then thought about the good that came out of each situation and felt grateful. For example, if I had an unsuccessful friendship, at least I learned what I do not want in a future friendship. I also tried to figure out what attracted me to that person in the first place and learn from that.

I quickly realized that my most "hurtful" interactions were the ones that taught me the most about life, about myself and what I wanted. After completing my list and writing out the lessons learned, I said each name out loud one-by-one, with the following words:

"I forgive you [**name of person**] for hurting me, and I thank you for giving me/teaching me/helping me with [**the positive outcome**]. "

This was one of the most liberating exercises for my heart. I felt so much lighter and happier after releasing so much disappointment and pent-up anger.

So please try to remember that when someone wrongs you, it is rarely personal. It is almost always highly contextual, but we don't always see or understand the full picture in the moment. We zoom in on our personal interpretation and forget that there is a second perspective or reasoning that might rationalize seemingly offensive behaviour.

Sometimes it feels like life is one of those quirky movie scenes where an old man yells at a woman buying flowers, because she bumped his leg. The backstory reveals that the man's wife fell ill that morning and was admitted to the hospital. He too was buying flowers for her but probably for the last time, which explains his overreaction to the bump. There is always a backstory - always.

The practice of releasing others is difficult, however, once completed, you'll feel lighter, happier, and better able to focus on your recovery!

Co-worker Negativity

Here is a personal story illustrating the importance of reframing our past in a positive light and the good it brought you.

Many years ago, I was let go from my job. I worked under a boss that was something other than amazing. I was shocked, hurt, and embarrassed by the whole situation, especially since I was also 6 months pregnant at the time.

It was especially painful to part with my colleagues and one in particular, who became my best friend while we worked together. Five years after I was let go, when people would ask how we met, I would explain that we bonded over a contentious work situation and then I would elaborate on the negative details.

The truth is that we bonded irrespective of our environment, bosses, or experiences at work. We bonded because we had great chemistry, engaging conversations, and enjoyed working alongside each other. We even won an award for a project we worked on together. So now, when people ask how we met, I eliminate the negative and focus on the best thing that happened to me at work - our friendship.

f) Exercise Physically & Mentally

If nothing else, engaging in one hour of physical activity a day is the single most important piece of advice I can give you. Exercise is medically proven to reduce fatigue, anxiety, stress, sleep problems and depression.[11] Moreover, exercise has been proven time and time again in hundreds of studies to reduce the side effects of chemotherapy[12]!

There are many ways to put this into action. Get moving by going outside and taking a walk - no need to make it too strenuous. A good brisk walk is just as good as anything to

---

[11] Mustian KM, Sprod LK, Janelsins M, Peppone LJ, Mohile S. Exercise Recommendations for Cancer-Related Fatigue, Cognitive Impairment, Sleep problems, Depression, Pain, Anxiety, and Physical Dysfunction: A Review. Oncol Hematol Rev. 2012;8(2):81-88.

[12] Singh B, Spence RR, Steele ML, Sandler CX, Peake JM, Hayes SC. A systematic review and meta-analysis of the safety, feasibility and effect of exercise in women with stage II+ breast cancer. Archives of Physical Medicine and Rehabilitation, May 2018. Arch Phys Med Rehabil. 2018 Dec;99(12):2621-2636.

boost your mood, lower blood sugar, lower cholesterol, improve heart health and many other benefits.

I wrote a song called "Moving," and one of the lines of the songs is "if you wanna move up, you gotta move, gotta move, move, move!" You can't be lazy about this and there are no shortcuts. Exercising to music is another option that makes the time pass more quickly with seemingly less effort.

Here are some ideas that can get you moving:

- Watch Zumba videos on YouTube and dance in your living room
- Go for a walk in your neighbourhood, either on your own or with a friend
- Go for a nature hike
- Walk around the mall (especially great when the weather is bad)

- Join a gym

- Invest in a treadmill or elliptical machine at home

- Go salsa dancing

- Run after your kids or pet for thirty minutes

- Play a video game that requires you to move, like Just Dance

- Play tennis, basketball, racquetball, swim or whatever sport moves you

Our brains also benefit from exercise. When our brains learn something new or engage in an activity such as a game, you are growing your mind's capacity to think and react positively to situations.

A study published in the Journal of the International Neuropsychology Society found that stimulating cognitive activities, such as doing crosswords, significantly delayed the onset of dementia in the elderly.[13]

There are many easily accessible tools and games that are available to exercise and sharpen your mind:

- Doing sudoku

- Solving crosswords

- Reading a book

- Assembling a puzzle

- Listening to a podcast lecture

- Using apps such as Lumosity

- Learning a new language

- Taking a new route to work

---

[13] Pillai, J., Hall, C., Dickson, D., Buschke, H., Lipton, R., & Verghese, J. (2011). Association of Crossword Puzzle Participation with Memory Decline in Persons Who Develop Dementia. Journal of the International Neuropsychological Society, 17(6), 1006-1013. doi:10.1017/S1355617711001111

g) Feed the Soul Through Prayer and Meditation

Call it religion, nature, or the energy of the universe, taking a moment every day to meditate or pray is powerful. In this way you can quiet your mind, achieve gratitude and focus on what your future self looks like.

During my year of treatments, I tried all different forms of prayer and meditation to determine what combination worked best for me. I found that prayer was extremely beneficial as an opportunity to say thank you and be grateful for all the blessings - both big and small - in my life.

I had a special prayer that I said every night over lit candles, asking that I be healed and blessed with a long life. I also took the opportunity to ask for anything specific that I needed and to express appreciation for all that I had.

In addition, I was not shy to ask people to pray for me. Whenever anyone asked, what can I do to help you? I responded, "Please pray for me!" I asked every Rabbi I knew to pray for me with their congregations.

I also found meditation very helpful. Often, on my most anxiety-filled nights, a ten-minute meditation was just as effective at putting me to sleep as the strongest medications. I discovered an app called Headspace that was very effective at calming my mind.

Another helpful technique I tried was Kundalini yoga. (Kundalini focuses on the health of the mind and spirit rather than building the body through traditional yoga poses. It involves getting in a pose, while reciting various songs and mantras over a period of five minutes to an hour, depending on the intended result.)

Engaging in Kundalini yoga helped me release emotional energy in a positive and uplifting way. Honing my mind in this way gave me perspective and an overall feeling of calm. There were many days that I had copious amounts of pent up emotional energy after a difficult treatment session. Afterwards, while engaging in a specific yoga pose or movement, I found the tears gently rolling down my face for fifteen minutes straight - all of this with a subtle smile on my face!

Overall, I felt better on the days I took ten minutes to pray, meditate or otherwise relax my mind. The anxiety and stress over the multitude of procedures I had to face were greatly reduced.

Faith Through Fire

Although the following story is about a community coming together in faith and prayer, it also relates to taking an

Aggressive Action of Love and Recruiting your Aggressively Positive Clan.

Over the last few years mass challah bakes became popular - sometimes including up to 2,000 women collectively making dough and praying. It was not uncommon for the Jewish community to hold a mass challah bake in support of someone's recovery from illness. The biblical commandment, or mitzvah (good deed), to bake holy braided bread was and continues to be incumbent upon women for the weekly Friday night Sabbath dinner.

I decided that I would mobilize my community to pray for me during a challah bake, shortly after my diagnosis as I embarked on treatment. Below I will go into a short explanation of what this special ritual entails:

The blessings, prayers and good energy put into the ingredients of the challah dough is what makes the process special. While adding sugar, you think about the sweetness you want in your life. Flour represents sustenance such as wealth and stability. Eggs embody fertility for those trying to get pregnant or trying to give birth to new projects. Oil anoints the family with holiness and yeast symbolizes growth. My favourite ingredient is salt, because it represents discipline in the home. It is traditional to hold back just a little bit on the salt as is required in the recipe, because when it comes to disciplinary words, sometimes a little less is more.

Before baking and eating the challah, a special blessing is said. As part of this blessing you can include prayers for anyone or anything as desired. Jewish women have used challah baking as a vehicle to focus their blessings and good intentions for thousands of years. Now I take you back to the story.

Through word of mouth only, with only four days' notice and the help of two Rabbis' wives, I was floored to see that over

400 women showed up in support of my challah bake in honour of my recovery.

Old high school classmates, my parents' friends and acquaintances, and even strangers showed up to make dough and pray for me. This unexpected and overwhelming show of support moved me to tears. I used the opportunity to pray and uplift myself, but also to uplift my gracious community with positive words and songs. Most guests walked in crying but left smiling.

(I must mention that on that same day of my Challah bake in Toronto, seventy women in Israel made up of friends and family made their own challah bake in support, that I got to watch via Facetime!)

It was overwhelming to receive so much love and I felt extremely fortunate to have such a giving network.

When I got home, I placed my ready -to-bake challah dough on a tray in the oven at the instructed 350° Fahrenheit temperature, and went upstairs to shower. I asked my husband Isaac to mind the oven while I was showering. My body was literally shaking from the energy I gave and received during the challah bake and I needed a good cleanse. I stepped into the shower and fell apart.

Sobbing and crying from deep within my heart and soul, I pleaded with G-d to show me the way. I begged that I should grow as a person as opposed to the cancerous growth in my body. I cried out loud that I couldn't make sense of what it all meant, and that I needed a sign - a big sign - to show me the way back to health.

The words barely left my lips when Isaac rushed into the bathroom. Out of breath and seemingly in a panic, he gasped, "Babe, you got to come see this, the house is full of smoke!"

Indeed, the upper floor was already becoming blanketed in swirling smoke. Our home was still relatively new and our freshly installed and tested smoke alarms had somehow failed to go off.

Hearts pounding, we raced downstairs. The smoke on the first floor was so thick that I couldn't even see the pot lights in the ceiling. Identifying the oven as the source of the fire, Isaac showed me the tray he had pulled out before turning it off and rushing upstairs. The challah had been baking for barely ten minutes.

There was a pronounced black ring around the challah, but amazingly nothing had happened to the challah itself - it was completely white. I even picked up the challah to check underneath and it was white along the bottom as well.

We took a few moments to reflect on what had happened. I took this visual as the sign I was seeking, seemingly in response to my pleading moments earlier in the shower. When Isaac asked, "What is the meaning of all of this?" I calmly replied, "G-d is putting me through a fire, and I will come out unscathed."

From that moment on, I had faith that everything would be ok.

h.) Create an Aggressively Positive Environment

Let's face it - we all live with imperfections in our home lives. We all have something to work on and improve, whether it be a challenge of the mind, body or soul. We try to surround ourselves with strong and positive people. However, we also need to remember that our physical environment has a deep impact on our overall well being and happiness. We find this concept in most religions. As my Rabbi Hildesheim always says, "Happiness brings blessings". If that is the case, being happy in your environment will also bring better outcomes in your life.

The objective here is to create a physical space that makes you happy. There are many aspects of your surroundings that can be changed with the goal of improving or boosting your spirit. Think of your own ideas by reflecting upon the places where you feel happiest, and then identify the items that stand out as being the cause of that happiness.

Here are some ideas to get you started:

- Recolour your walls with a new coat of paint; try calming tones like blues and greens or energizing yellows and reds!

- Declutter a room, or even start with one drawer! Dump everything on your bed, keep only what is good and useful or makes you happy. Donate or throw out the rest!

- Accent your living area with a pair of throw pillows in your favourite colour

- Hang artwork that brings you inspiration or joy.

- Feng shui the placement of your current furniture (a Chinese tradition of harmonizing individuals with their surroundings).

- Add flowers or plants to your surroundings - even a small bouquet of flowers livens up a neutral space.

- Light candles, incense, and salt lamps to help bring a sense of calm to any room.

- Introduce a colourful area rug to boost the energy in a room.

For more ideas, search YouTube or Pinterest for some affordable do-it-yourself home improvement projects that are not too energy intensive. Some keywords you can type into the search bar to get you started are DIY Furniture, DIY Art, DIY Sculptures, or similar terms. The possibilities are endless.

I personally enjoy seeing a rainbow of colour everywhere and chose my decor items accordingly. I also make sure to have an iPad or computer with speakers near me so that I can easily listen to music or engage in online meditation or a Zumba video.

Listen to yourself and remember that there are no right or wrong answers. Your space influences your mood every day, and if you are on the journey of Aggressive Positivity, improving that space will help you tremendously.

STEP 3: DEFLECTING NEGATIVITY

There is no light without dark. No hot without cold. And of course, positivity is constantly opposed by negativity.

It can be tremendously easy to be swayed by negativity, seeing how it so readily permeates our lives. Every day, news broadcasts and websites are inundated with stories of bad news. Our social media networks excel at amplifying negative thoughts and messages across the globe with dizzying speed and effectiveness.

Our success in practicing Aggressive Positivity hinges on our ability to deal with negative thoughts and emotions. Let's explore how.

Acknowledge Your Negative Thoughts

Negative thoughts are uncontrollable - we all have them. Without judgement of ourselves, we need to be aware of our thoughts and recognize the negativity when it arises. Who or what thought is bringing you down? Once you identify the source or root cause, give the negativity space to process, both physically and mentally.

Negative thoughts can come into your mind like a cloud and can often linger. It is important to recognize that it is okay that the thoughts entered in the first place - we are human after all - but eventually they will blow away like a storm, or you can learn to take shelter. Let me share a few techniques.

When you have a negative thought, here are a few strategies to help process it:

- As discussed previously, separate fact from fiction. Ask yourself: is what I am worried about just a fabricated worry in my head, or is it truly justified?

- If it is justified, it is OK to feel sad, nervous, upset, anxious, or angry. The only way to flip an emotion is to allow it to enter and give it space in the first place. It is very normal to feel many different emotions in difficult situations. Don't be afraid to cry. It is human and it is necessary. Only after you feel it, can you let it go.

- Check in with your emotions after an hour, after a day, and after a week. Elements of what you were feeling will change. Take note of what got better and what remained.

- If you are feeling ready, try a mind flip! See the previous chapters about how to perform mind flips. (Go to Mind Flip Examples)

Distance Yourself from Negativity

Beware of negative people

While we deal with negativity in our own minds and environments, the same practice must be applied to negativity from other people.

During my teenage years, a close friend of mine yelled at me badly during an argument. She was going through a very stressful time and decided to take out some pent-up aggression on me. I called my dad at work and explained what had just happened through bursts of tears.

It's hard to remember what my friend and I argued about now, however, my Father's response made a deep impression on me. I call this Johnyism, "The Jungle."

119

He said: "There are many animals in the jungle. There is the gentle giraffe and the brave lion, the turtle and the hyena. Today, your friend barked like a hyena, but that doesn't mean she doesn't deserve her place in the jungle. "

Those words instantly put things in perspective. We cannot expect people to be what they are not, but we can still try to be the best version of ourselves within our control. Every animal has their role to play within the jungle - the gazelles eat grass, the lions eat gazelles, and the vultures clean up the leftovers. Each animal was born and raised to play a role - and humans are no different!

My negative feelings dissipated quickly, and I began applying the principle in my everyday life. The philosophy of accepting people as who and what they are (even if they are temporarily acting out of character) has granted me additional perspective and wisdom that helps me navigate relationships, especially in difficult times.

Specifically, the idea of The Jungle helps me avoid being judgemental, to try and understand where people are coming from, removing myself from situations where necessary. There is always a back story to every single person's behaviour. Everyone was raised by different parents, with different skills and customs, in a different environment at a different moment in time. "Everyone is battling something or going through something hard" (lyrics from Alive). (Not everyone has the best coping or survival tools and we are all different animals that think and act differently.

That being said, if you are in a state of needing to be uplifted and healed, you cannot spare any of your precious energy and you need to avoid giving it away to people that bring you down. To draw upon a jungle analogy: animals have territories in their ecosystems for a reason. When a gazelle is injured, it naturally avoids going into treacherous areas out of its territory that will put it in further danger. It will find a safe area with shelter in order to recover. Animals inherently understand their boundaries, and we should too!

It is important to reiterate that in a challenging situation you need to focus your energy on yourself and not judge the animals (people) for who they naturally are. Choose to be surrounded with the animals (people) that align with your need for positivity.

Communicating your specific needs regarding Aggressive Positivity to friends or family isn't easy. Again, remember that the situation is only temporary. Be strong in voicing your desire for positive information, and don't be ashamed to speak up when you hear negative sentiments being vocalized around you.

So, when you hear well-meaning sentiments like, "what are the side effects of your medication?", "are you going to be ok?" or "I heard the surgery is terrible," use all your strength to avoid engaging. It is perfectly fine to respond, "I don't know, or want to know. I only want to know good things," or, "I would rather talk about other things." If you can manage to say that with a smile, it can eliminate the potential awkwardness and reinforce your desire for positivity to whoever you are conversing with. When someone genuinely smiles at you, it is difficult not to smile back!

Some people feel the need to dwell on the negative side. This tendency could be a genetic biological predisposition, a personality type, or an unfortunate side effect from a difficult life challenge that has sucked up their energy and ability to think any other way. Their negativity is not necessarily their fault and certainly not yours. However, because you are within the throes of an aggressive challenge, you cannot allow your energy to be spent on their negativity.

If they cannot engage in a positive way - for whatever reason - politely and discreetly limit your time with them. This is just so that you can keep your strength while in the healing process. Your tolerance for negativity will be much stronger once you are in a better place personally, after having overcome your challenge.

Beware of the Internet

We are fortunate to live in a time and place where unfettered access to the internet is widely available. We can easily tap into endless streams of information and communicate with the entire world from our pocket-sized devices. Keeping that in mind, we owe it to ourselves to consume content with a keenly critical eye.

We are all guilty of selectively reading negative reviews before making online purchases. In fact, we now know scientifically that reading negative reviews has a greater impact on our purchasing decisions than positive reviews.[14] Perhaps this phenomenon happens because we, as humans, tend to dwell on what could go wrong. Or, as especially observed in healthcare, we want to fully understand all the information and associated risks before deciding. All the

---

[14] The Effect of Word of Mouth on Sales: Online Book Reviews. Judith A. Chevalier and Dina Mayzlin, Journal of Marketing Research 2006 43:3, 345-354.

while we can forget that the quality and accuracy of negative reviews can be as questionable as positive ones.

So, when we browse information about our conditions, medications, or prognoses online, it is critical to maintain a sceptical view about what you read, especially when the author is neither credible nor verifiable.

In the spirit of Aggressive Positivity, we also need to understand that negative content is much more commonplace than positive. Studies have shown that customers with a negative service experience are more likely to post a negative review as opposed to a positive review from a satisfied customer.[15] Maybe this happens simply because a satisfied customer is satisfied, and has no need to let out their frustration!

---

[15] Yoo, K. & Gretzel, U. (2008). What motivates consumers to write online travel reviews?. Information Technology & Tourism, 10 (4), 283-295.

Moreover, personal context will overwhelmingly dictate peoples' online contribution, especially as it relates to medical discussions. This means that you will rarely, if ever, find someone that shares your exact same medical situation. There are countless factors that shape your reality, such as age, weight, shape, health, lifestyle, location, culture, socioeconomic situation, family construct, mental state of mind, and access to medicine - and each one can have a significant impact on your outcome. When you read about someone's reaction to a specific drug, treatment, or procedure, you are probably learning about a specific person's worst-case scenario that does not remotely apply to you.

Giving birth is a good analogy for this idea. When you are pregnant, everyone rushes to tell you about their birthing horror story, but that is not and will not be *your* story. Birthing experiences vary wildly, and no two stories are exactly alike.

That is why, in my case, I chose to trust my oncologist when it came to medical advice. After meeting her in person, I connected with her and my intuition told me to trust her. She knew me, my body, my particular situation, and I saw her as the Sherpa on my journey. I directed all my questions and concerns to her, since only she knew my specifics.

I was also fortunate enough to have a common type of cancer that is treated in a standard way. So, I didn't need to spend too much time researching treatment alternatives. If the situation was different, I would choose reputable institutions for my research. I got second and third opinions from doctors, and that was enough for me. I asked all my treatment partners to avoid telling me survival rates, recurrence rates, side effects or even what "stage" my disease reached. I also avoided learning the exact names of my medications so it wouldn't tempt me into Googling the side effects.

Even today, I do not know the full names of the chemo drugs I was on - I only know it was dose dense AC-T. For me, diving into detailed medical information would be too negative, and it would be too difficult not to dwell on every detail or possible outcome, effectively making me crazy.

This kind of "chosen ignorance" isn't for everyone. Some do the exact opposite; there is no one "right" way to navigate a life challenge. Some find the detailed knowledge of every aspect calming. I am the complete opposite, which is why I personally preferred going in slightly blind.

The objective here is to be aware of the possible negativity in the information and not let it impact your mindset. You have to be able to sift through the contextual noise and get the information you are after. If you do not feel clear-headed enough but still feel the need to know more, consider reading information provided by a trusted source such as your hospital, doctors office, or support group/charity organization related to your situation rather than browsing random content online.

Distraction from Negative Situations

Sometimes we find ourselves in unsavoury situations that we simply cannot avoid, like receiving a four-hour chemo treatment, or sitting with a crying child. These situations don't improve instantaneously and another way we can get through them is through various techniques of redirection and distraction.

As mentioned earlier, music is a powerful tool you can use to more easily navigate a challenging life situation. Music can also be used as an audio cue for action. We should take advantage of this important tool during our journey of Aggressive Positivity.

In Pavlov's famous experiment demonstrating classical conditioning, he exposed dogs to a bell sound right before offering them food. Eventually they reacted physiologically to the sound of the bell by salivating.[16] In a similar way, we can condition our minds to involuntarily react positively to music. In fact, most of us are already hardwired to relax and improve our mood when listening to a favourite song.

Music is just one example of distraction. In fact, a 2012 study published in Psychological Science found that participants reported reduced discomfort when they were asked to perform a distracting mental test as a painful stimulus was delivered to their arms.[17]

Even more interesting, a separate study proved that the power of distraction provided positive neurological effects in addition to psychological benefits. Participants were asked to perform a simple or difficult mental task while a controlled amount of heat was applied to their arms. The results showed that the group that performed the harder of the two memory

[16] Pavlov, I. P. (1927/1960). Conditional Reflexes. New York: Dover Publication

[17] Buhle, J. T., Stevens, B. L., Friedman, J. J., & Wager, T. D. (2012). Distraction and Placebo: Two Separate Routes to Pain Control. Psychological Science, 23(3), 246–253. https://doi.org/10.1177/0956797611427919

tasks reported they perceived less pain because of the distraction. What's more, their less painful experience was reflected by lower activity in the spinal cord as observed by MRI scans.[18]

Below I give some great examples of distractions that are easy to find and use. Whatever you find most effective to distract your mind, make it a habit.

Here are some ideas I loved:

- Search "satisfying videos" on YouTube. My kids taught me this one. These videos show interesting objects being squished or manipulated - like spaghetti coming out of a pasta machine.

[18] Christian Sprenger, Falk Eippert, Jürgen Finsterbusch, Ulrike Bingel, Michael Rose, Christian Büchel. Attention Modulates Spinal Cord Responses to Pain. Current Biology, 2012; DOI: 10.1016/j.cub.2012.04.006

- Nature videos of animals can be good for relaxation and perspective.

- Play Bedazzled, BlockPuzzle and other similarly repetitive and totally addictive games on your phone.

- Podcasts: search any topic, find a lecture that appeals to you and learn something!

- TED talks are my favourite because they are filtered for you. They seek out the most interesting subject matter experts that share new ways of thinking, new research and astounding beauty in talks that range from three to thirty minutes, on a wide variety of topics. (It's one of my bucket list dreams to give a talk on Aggressive Positivity!)

- Play Sudoku, do a crossword or similar challenging mind game.

- Play cards, chess, or any board game.

- Listen to a playlist on iTunes or Spotify to suit your musical taste.

- Watch an online Kaleidoscope video

You can use these tricks to relax yourself when in a nerve-wracking moment, and they are also useful to help with sleep or for simple entertainment.

Working out has a similar mind distraction or focusing effect. The natural endorphins released in your body will put you in a better state of mind. Although, working out is not always a possibility depending on the situation you are in.

Let me share a few distraction stories.

The Brushing Teeth Dance

Right after my mastectomy surgery, I could lift my arm to about 60 degrees, maximum. The doctors prescribed a heavy regiment of exercises in order to regain my range of motion. The exercises required me to stretch my arm to the point of pain. I diligently counted down the seconds for the duration of each of the exercises, taking a total of 45 minutes, three times a day.

I dreaded these exercises simply because they felt painful. I forced myself anyways and then my body would begin to shake uncontrollably from the pain, not allowing me to continue. I made slow progress, but not nearly enough. Two weeks went by and I was forced to postpone a pre-radiation planning CT scan because my arm couldn't reach the harness of the scanner.

I thought about this the next morning while brushing my teeth. To help my mood, I put on some Zumba music. Of course, if you know me at all, it was unsurprising that the beats prompted me to do a kind of hip-gyrating brushing teeth dance. For some reason, I decided to try some of my exercises in the midst of my gyrations. I noticed that I could push myself harder and farther because I was having fun and my mind was off the pain that the stretches normally caused.

Needless to say, this became my new way of doing the exercises and managed to make more progress in 2 weeks than I had in 6 weeks post-surgery.

The lesson here is that if you can distract your mind from pain, you can achieve more. Music is truly a great distractor.

Somewhere Over the Rainbow

During one of my CAT scans at the hospital, I noticed an elderly man whimpering in the scan prep area, while having an IV inserted. The nurse was on her third attempt at trying to find a suitable vein, in which to inject the needle.

I politely introduced myself to the man, explaining that I am a singer and asked, "Would it help put your mind at ease if I sang you a song? What's your favourite kind of music?" He replied that he loves the old classics, so I started singing "Somewhere Over the Rainbow." Halfway through the song, the nurse smiled as she tapped his arm with pride and said, "you're done!"

The man was completely shocked. He went on to exclaim, "But I felt nothing!" The nurse proceeded to jokingly offer me a job in the ward, calming patients by singing.

Karaoke Chemo

Similar to how my singing distracted a patient from a painful IV insertion, I used music to distract myself during chemo treatments. I knew that this technique was effective since I sang my way through most of my labour contractions (through three births!), so I figured it would work during chemotherapy as well.

I have a talent for singing in languages that I don't speak, so during many of the four-hour long treatments, I would listen to and learn new songs, often in different languages. I was usually one of the last patients in the ward, so at the end of appointments I often sang karaoke with my dad or one of the nurses in their different native tongues. I was singing for the nurses in Serbian, Tagalog, Greek, and even Mandarin.

It made all of us laugh, and I can dare to say that I even enjoyed some of the chemotherapy experience. I dreamed of having a private room with a portable karaoke machine wheeled in with mics, so I could have a Karaoke Chemo Party. Hey, a girl can dream!

CONCLUSION

I realize that the approach of Aggressive Positivity is not for everyone. It requires you to be "all in" to reap serious results. I am convinced that for me, practicing Aggressive Positivity made the difference between life and death.

Success requires swift and aggressive effort from a mental and physical standpoint. Basically, it's a serious commitment; only YOU can make happen, and that responsibility is solely yours. You can recruit a clan to support you on your journey, but the majority of the effort remains yours.

Let me go over the key concepts for you one last time:

Step 1: Flip Your Mind

Separate fact from fiction, and flip the negative challenge into something positive, for example, "I'm not sick, I'm healing."

Step 2: Perform Aggressive Actions of Love

Take an aggressive action of love to support your new positive outlook. Schedule what you love aggressively, such that you are continuously looking forward to something that fuels you. Then you will have the energy to keep your thoughts positive, and your challenge will fade in impact and importance.

Step 3: Deflect Negativity

Heal the negativity within yourself, while taking a step back from negative environments and people when possible. Build yourself an environment that can allow you to grow and heal. Repeat these steps over and over and over.

Remember, use the tools within your grasp, and don't forget the power of community, music, exercise, prayer, meditation, and laughter.

Good luck!

Join the conversation about Aggressive Positivity:

Facebook:

www.facebook.com/aggressivepositivity

Instagram:

@aggressivepositivityofficial

APPENDIX

Thinking Behind Aggressive Actions of Love

I wanted to share some background on how I came to understand the importance of actions in shaping the future.

My thirst for positive action as a necessary component to support positive thoughts is rooted and influenced by the Jewish concept for luck, or in Hebrew, "Mazal." You hear it all the time when people say, "Mazal tov on the marriage of your son," or, "Mazal tov on your graduation!"

Translated very literally, mazal tov means "luck good." "Mazal" means "luck" and "tov" means "good." However, the Hebrew word for luck is very different from the English word, as it has nothing to do with coincidence but is an acronym for something else! Let me explain.

141

The Hebrew language works with consonants that function as the letters, and the vowels sit above or below each consonant. The word "mazal" is written in the Hebrew-English equivalent letters "MZL" with accompanying vowels. Each of the three letters stand for something else:

M = Makom = Place

Z = Zman = Time

L = La'asot = Action

So, the Hebrew word for luck breaks down into a function of "Be at the right PLACE, at the right TIME, and take ACTION!"[19] This is how luck is formed - through action.

To illustrate, if you're going to play the lottery, you actually have to physically buy the ticket first. This Jewish concept is

---

[19] Let's Ask the Rabbi, by Raymond Apple, p16.

very deeply entrenched in my psyche. It helps me feel like I have a measure of control in my life, in that I can take action to affect my daily reality. If I don't feel lucky, or things are not going in the direction I want, I have *three* different avenues to explore and improve my world: change my physical or mental "PLACE," change the TIMING or take different ACTIONS to affect a new outcome.

The Diagnosis Details

I thought some readers would be interested or curious to understand some of the nitty gritty details of what I went through medically. I never chose to talk about these details at the time of my treatment, and even now do not enjoy writing about them. But I do want to give hope to those going through something similar, knowing that I came out on top.

I found my tumour myself after feeling a small (about 2 centimetres) semi-hard mass in the middle of my right breast that didn't go away with my monthly cycle. My family physician sent me for an ultrasound, and the doctor at the local clinic told me, "I don't like what I see, and I have never been wrong in all my years of practice."

Two weeks later, they performed a biopsy of my breast and lymph nodes. A day after that, they confirmed that I had locally advanced breast cancer. My tumour was hormone receptor (HR) negative and estrogen receptor (ER) positive. I don't know and never knew what "stage" the cancer was at. I never knew and still do not know the survival rates, recurrence rates, or other statistics associated with my type of cancer.

I had every test in the books done to me. Blood tests, CT scans, MRIs, ECGs, blood volume tests, bone density scans, you name it. At one point we had a major scare since the doctors suspected the cancer had spread to my bones and liver. The same day they delivered my chemo treatment schedule, they let me know that I had a little birthmark on my liver and masses on my hip bones that were in fact benign "bone islands."

They put in a peripherally inserted central catheter (PICC) in my left arm for easier direct administration of drugs, blood withdrawal, and chemo medication. The insertion procedure was painless and done under local anaesthetic. The reason I needed a PICC was because the chemo I had was very good at destroying blood vessels. I had to carefully wrap my arm with layers of saran wrap before showering in order not to wet the PICC. I also could not swim with the PICC inserted. The PICC remained in my arm for four months until my last chemo treatment. By the way, it was shockingly painless to have the PICC removed, it literally slid out of my arm like butter.

I completed eight rounds of AC-T dose dense chemotherapy, four hours each time, which landed me in the hospital with heart palpitations after the sixth round. In general, my side effects were mild. I was more tired than usual, experienced some mental fogginess, but overall, I had a good experience. I did lose all my hair. I developed some nerve damage and numbness (neuropathy) in my hands and toes from my last rounds of chemo. I never completely recovered full strength in my hands.

After 24 hours following each round of chemo, I needed a needle to the stomach to administer medication that prevented my antibody levels from dipping too low.

After completing Chemo, I had a needle once a month to shut down my ovaries until I could get them surgically removed. This was to eliminate estrogen levels in my body, since my disease ate that for dinner.

After chemo, I had a right-side mastectomy and lymph node dissection. I had two drains post-surgery. One came out after ten days and the second after three weeks. I developed a skin infection a week after surgery that required a visit to the hospital and was taken care of with antibiotics.

Post-surgery pathology showed diseased cells fifteen centimetres across my breast tissue and seventeen of the nineteen lymph nodes they removed were affected by cancer. As well, there were diseased cells too close to my skin. This prompted my radiation oncologist to order a boost to my skin, in addition to the 25 rounds of localized radiation. I had to delay radiation by two weeks because the post-surgery stiffness in my arm prevented it from reaching the right position in the radiation machine harness, high above my shoulder.

I used music and CBD oil to alleviate the pain while completing the exercises and stretches to achieve the necessary range of motion. I refused to take painkillers (Oxycontin, as suggested by my surgeon) before my exercises, because it took me three days of crying around the clock to get myself off them post mastectomy surgery.

I had five weeks of radiation every day during the week and a break on the weekends. Each session lasted an hour because after the usual dose, they put a ⅓-inch thick silicone "skin" on my body and gave me another dose. The silicone layer would trick the machine into applying the radiation directly to my skin.

Post radiation treatment every day, I applied my dad's homemade topical aloe and vitamin concoction that helped ease the burning sensation and minimize major scarring. The major side effect of radiation was a deep level of exhaustion. A week after the last treatment, all my skin bubbled and peeled off. The tiredness peaked in the first few months following my last treatment and it took a full year to start to feel my energy come back.

Three months after completing radiation, I had preventative surgery to remove my ovaries and fallopian tubes. That surgery was the easiest of all my procedures. It was laparoscopic - a minimally invasive technique using small incisions and a bigger one through the belly button. Afterwards, I had some pain in my joints for a few days because of trapped gas in my body that was later reabsorbed.

I did have some major psychological setbacks at the one-year anniversaries of all the milestone moments of my treatments, requiring five sessions with a psychologist specializing in oncological patients. Despite my best efforts, I did develop mild PTSD from my experiences.

It took two years of dedicated and often painful hard work at the gym to achieve symmetry in my movements again. It also took me two years to wean myself off gabapentin, a medication used to ease nerve pain from neuropathy and damaged nerves from surgery. I had upper arm numbness and at the surgery site for two years (nerves can typically take years to regenerate and stop misfiring). Today, I occasionally feel jolts here and there, but I am thankful they are not ongoing.

I am now in full menopause and love how my moods are more consistent. Sadly, I am not a good candidate for breast reconstructive surgery for several medical reasons. Firstly, I lost skin elasticity due to the radiation. I am thin and would need to gain 30 pounds in order to fashion a breast from my own stomach tissue. Doing that would require taking my entire stomach (versus half for most people) and two arteries to feed the tissue (versus the usual one artery). This doubles my risk for complications as the arteries can close on the way up (this happened to two women close to me) and the surgery becomes 12 versus the usual 8 hours of surgery. Combine this with the nerve damage It took two years to recover from, re-opening the same scar and a risk of chronic pain for the rest of my life and the decision was easy. Until they learn to grow a "boob in a tube," I will be happy to live life with one breast.

I still take a dose of Letrozole every day to shut down estrogen production in the fat cells in my body. I also take vitamin D and Calcium. I receive a Zoledronic Acid treatment in the Chemo ward, every six months. It is an IV treatment that takes a few hours, that fills in the porosity in my bones to prevent osteoporosis. I am still watched very closely by my medical team.

151

Acknowledgements

First and foremost, I would like to thank my dear husband Isaac Zisckind. You held down the fort during my year of treatments so that I could fly on my cloud. I love you and appreciate everything you did and continue to do!

To my wonderful children Gabriella, Eliana and Aviya - thank you for your endless smiles, hugs, optimism, and willingness to go along with Ima's crazy ideas. I love you endlessly.

Thank you to my parents, Betty & John Twena, who accompanied me to every single appointment and treatment and supported me in every way imaginable. I love beyond.

To my siblings and their spouses Allon & Noa Twena, Adi & Tania Twena, and Shira & Shay Shapira, thank you for your continuous stream of calls, visits, accompanying me to appointments, jokes, videos, hugs, love, advice and fun times every single day!

Thank you to my in-laws Millie & Moti Zisckind and Sandy & Jeremy Diamond for your dedication, selflessness, and support in all situations. I appreciate and love you very much.

Thank you to my insanely and amazingly supportive extended family that gave and continue to give me energy and love every single day: Bubbie Elaine Melnick, Eli & Rivka Melnick, Doron Melnick & Shana Haberman, Micha & Lisa Melnick, Adam Melnick, Doda Alicia Shelemay, Dita & Stan Kramer, Daphy Kramer, Dana Daly, Maya Kramer, Daniel Kramer, Natalie Kramer, Koby & Yael Twena, Liad Twena, Morane Twena, Edan Twena, Ori Twena, Michal & Koby Even, Yarden Even, Golan Even, Yamit Even, Sharon Even, and Sharon Bachar.

153

Thank you to my partner in crime, my talented cousin Michael Melnick. This is our second book writing adventure together; the first being <u>By My Mother's Hand: our grandfathers' holocaust memoir</u>. Thank you for your conscientious and heartfelt editing skills and ubiquitous Pegasus ways. Thank you for the endless hours, encouragement, quiet support and mapping my book in a 3D octopus-like moving chart! Also, thank you for connecting me with Dr. Adam Palanica who expertly found study sources to back my claims that added an air of sophistication to the book.

Thank you Rony Freiman of ShapeMediaDesigns for donating your time and talent in bringing my logo drawn on a napkin to life with flare, and the gorgeous cover design!

I also want to recognize my friends, that are too many to list. You know who you are. You were beside me throughout my journey. You gave me support, time, gifts and love that helped me get through my hardest moments. You amazing people walked and talked with me, gave me advice, tickled my head, prayed for me, sat by my bed as I recovered, made me insane art, dropped off food and care packages, baked challahs from afar, accompanied me to the hospital, donated time to help me with my videos, writing and music projects, encouraged me to write, taught me Kundalini Yoga, travelled with me and celebrated with me. I am also grateful to you for being amazing neighbours, providing medical advice, and providing your expertise. I thank you and love you all. Most importantly, you gave me your love and made me laugh, and for that I am truly grateful and blessed.

I'd like to thank the following people in alphabetical order for donating their time to help make my musical dreams come true:

Ido Adan, Victoria Barrie, Taras Blyzniuk, Diego Carreon, Natalie Chung, Kayla Diamond, Marny Florence, Monica Gold, Marla Joy, Ryan Krieser, Ashlyn Kuy, Shani Langzam, Jody Litvack, Karine Martin, Lindsay McBride, Michael Nissim, Lianne Tammi.

I want to make a special mention of people outside of my friendship circle who went out of their way to give me medical, spiritual or other types of support: Rebbetzin Chana Leah Bekerman, Rabbi Chaim Hildesheim, Rebbetzin Chanie Hildesheim, Dr. Darren Kagal, Dr. Zel Krajden, Mira Leshem, Dr. Cherine Salem, Mary Grace Cadion, and Carina Gloria.

A special shoutout goes to the doctors, nurses and staff at Sunnybrook Hospital, to whom I owe my life:

To Dr. Ellen Warner, I don't have the words to describe what you gave to me! Thank you for going along with all my Aggressive Positivity and giving me wings to fly. Thank you for always listening and never rushing out of the room, but mostly for giving me hope. I am amazed by what you do every single day and am convinced you are not of this planet!

Media

Below find various media related to Aggressive Positivity and my music :

Blogs

Suarez, A.L. (2017). Mom Goes For First Chemo Treatment. 3 Days Later, She Pens Emotional Song About Cancer Journey [Web Log]. Retrieved from https://www.littlethings.com/moms-song-about-cancer-alive-limore

Valente, J. C. (2017, June 8) 'Alive' Is the Perfect Anthem for Anyone Who's Suffered from an Illness or Disability [Web Log]. Retrieved from https://www.kveller.com/alive-is-the-perfect-anthem-for-anyone-whos-suffered-from-an-illness-or-disability/amp/

Live Again Project (2017, September 8)"AGGRESSIVE POSITI]VITY ™"— A singer/songwriter's mantra in her journey with breast cancer…the Live Again Story of Limore Twena [Web Log] Retrieved from https://medium.com/live-again-project/aggressive-positivity-a-live-again-mantra-from-singer-songwriter-limore-twena-b7e853dbc2b8

Newspapers

Minuk, S. (2018) Singer Channels Aggressive Positivity on New Album" Canadian Jewish News, Toronto, 22 August. Accessed https://www.cjnews.com/culture/entertainment/singer-channels-aggressive-positivity-on-new-album

Podcast & Blogger Interviews

Witz Education (2020, March) How To Become UNBREAKABLE and Overcome ADVERSITY! Accessed https://youtu.be/Sk1zYVAEoCo

Momjo Bloggers (2017, Otober 26) Aggressive Positivity with Singer and Cancer Survivor Limore. Accessed https://youtu.be/mSkzP9KGM5Q

Television

CP24 (August 2018) Jamie Gutfreund interviews Limore to promote her Toronto Concert https://www.cp24.com/video?clipId=1455690

i24 News (April 2018) Maya Kramer interviews Limore about Aggressive Positivity and her music https://www.facebook.com/maya.kramershahar/videos/2240286672648944?sfns=mo

i24 News (2017, July) Maya Kramer interviews Limore about Aggressive Positivity
https://www.facebook.com/watch/?v=873940439424624

Music

YouTube "Limore" Channel

> Alive (music video)
> Alive The Concert by Limore (Toronto)
> Alive The Concert in TLV
> It's Over (music video)
> Oleshe (music video that went viral on Facebook)
> Limore Takes Off Wig at Charity Event

iTunes

Alive by Limore (Full Album)
Oleshe by Limore

Radio

CBC Radio interview with Gill Deacon: "Song that came out of one uber ride". https://www.cbc.ca/listen/live-radio/1-82-here-and-now-toronto/clip/15745953-the-song-that-came-out-of-one-toronto-uber-ride

Documentary

Shine for Suzanne. (2017) "Rising from The Flames"
https://www.facebook.com/watch/?v=666647796862821

Song Lyrics to Alive the Album

Photo: Eli Amon Photography
Cover Design: Diego Carreon

ALIVE

(Limore, Kayla Diamond)

Written 2 days after my first chemo treatment

Everyone Is battling something
Or going through something hard
Everybody's got to fight
Everybody's got to try

No winners and no losers
No room for wrong or right
Never a place for judgement
Cause this is now our time

Chorus:
All this time I've been waiting for a sign
To show me the way, to show me the light
I feel free, just look at me
I'm alive, I'm alive, I'm alive
I'm alive, I'm alive, I'm alive

I fell asleep afraid and I woke up a lion
I put on my shield and I stand in the fire
I walk out unscathed
I'm untouchable today
I'm a warrior, protected and safe

Chorus:
All this time …

161

BURNING LIGHTS

(Limore, Kayla Diamond, Shira Shapira)

My most personal song, written at the height of my vulnerability after going completely bald

I feel so bare, no more secrets to share
Like a lonely wick, waiting to be lit
I'm hoping for more
Hoping there is something in the sky
To lift me up, to lift me up

I feel so unclothed, waiting to be born
To find my strength again
Sometimes you get blindsided
To change your ways
But I pick myself up again

CHORUS
Burnin lights shine on me
Show me the way, the way to be
I light a candle carefully
Every night I pray, I pray for me

I feel so bare, all my secrets were shared and
My lonely wick is burning, I'm on fire
I've hopin' and dreamin' and prayin'
Waiting for the day that
My fire will shine all over me

Burnin' lights shine on me
Show me the way, the way to be
I light a candle carefully
Every night I pray, I pray for me

My tears keep fallin' down on me
The lights are shinin', they dry up these tears
They're telling me quiet, it's gonna be OK
It doesn't matter what they say anyways

Burning lights, they shine
Burning lights shine on me

163

THINK GOOD

(Limore, Kayla Diamond)

Old man Joe was down on his luck
His wife is gone with another man
But he don't care
He's good on his own
A cigar and a scotch in his hand

It's a rainy day for little Renee
Her white t-shirt is turning gray
But she don't care, she's got more to spare
She knows that the world can wait

Chorus:
You gotta think good
To feel good
To be good in this life
It doesn't matter what it is
It doesn't matter who you are
It's alright

Grumpy Ray was mad all day
She married him anyways
What you don't know
Behind closed doors
Ray's got a gentle way

Chorus:
You gotta think good…

TEAR ME DOWN

(Limore, Kayla Diamond)
Written to give strength while facing adversity

My head is spinning, my hearts on the floor
I'm scared and I'm waiting for what's at my door
I haven't done anything wrong or unfair
My enemies are waiting, and I try not to care

Chorus:
Go ahead and try
Try to tear me down
Go ahead and try
Try to make a scene
I ain't going anywhere at all
You just helped me up my game
So please go ahead and try

You're so busy runnin, like a rat trapped in a cage
You can't see the bigger picture, 'Cuz for you its all the same
It's so easy rising high, when I'm building something tall
Like a skyscraper of metal, never bending ever tall

Chorus:
Go ahead and try…

I ain't go I ain't goin anywhere at all
I ain't go I ain't goin anywhere at all

ALL THE SAME

(Limore)

Written for my children

A butterfly has landed in my heart, it
Changed my life, a brand-new start
I will never see my life again
The way it was before you came

I will love you all the same
I will love you just the way you came, cause
I have loved you from the start
You will always have a place inside my heart

A butterfly has landed in my heart
Gave me courage from the start
Brought the colour to my life again
Spread your wings and fly away

Your love has made me who I am
I always knew there was a bigger plan
Cuz I have loved you from the start
Promise me we'll never ever be apart

I will love you all the same
I will love you just the way you came

You will love me , I will love you
I will love all the same

THANK YOU

(Limore, Kayla Diamond)

Inspired by Kayla's selflessness and all those that helped me climb a mountain

You put aside your ways, you opened up your heart for days
Sat and listened to the keys for a floatin' melody
You let me cry, you let me be
You are a rockstar and a queen

Chorus:
I wanna thank you for givin' me the best of you
I wanna thank you for givin' me your all
I wanna thank you, you never wanted anything
And you were there for me

Now I have my dream, an album full of songs to sing
Now I have it all and thanks to you I'll never fall
You let me cry, you let me be
You are a rockstar and a queen

I wanna thank you
For bringing out the best of me
I wanna thank you
For givin' me some soul
I wanna thank you
You never wanted anything
And you were there for me
And you were there for me

IT'S OVER

(Limore, Shira Shapira)

Written on my last day of radiation, on the booklet with information detailing all the side effects

Day after day, walkin with a smile
Knowing that this journey's gonna be awhile
Night after night prayin for the way
To open up my world so I can say
The future's looking bright, everything's going right
I've got all my plans worked out for me

Chorus:
Cuz It's over, never going back
Looking forward to all the things I'll do
Cause it's over, I get my life again and
I've finally found my purpose in the end

Day after day feelin in my heart
Everything will be a distant memory
Night after night, holding your hand
I needed you here and now I understand
I'll fill up my world with positivity
I've got bigger plans for humanity

Chorus:
Cuz It's over ...

Don't be discouraged by the road ahead

Its twisted it's turning just as I said
Every delay is OK you see
I need Aggressive Positivity to drive to me to greatness
With hope I sing a song for the present and future
Welcome to my new reality
And this is just the start, the start, the start

Chorus:
Cuz it's over…

PHOTOS

Recording Alive

2nd Challah Bake prior to mastectomy surgery

April 2017
Photo: Eli Melnick

May 2017 Singing at Gala 2 days before surgery
Photo: Justine Apple Photography

TRENDING ALIVE: AN ANTHEM FOR FACING THE ODDS
i24

June 2017 i24 News Interview

August 2018 "Alive the Concert Toronto"
Photo: Eli Melnick

April 2019 "Alive the Concert" Tel Aviv
Photo:

February 2020

Made in the USA
Monee, IL
01 May 2020